ERUPTION TO HOPE

ERUPTION TO HOPE

by Jean Vanier

GRIFFIN HOUSE

TORONTO 1971

© Jean Vanier, 1971

Hard Cover Edition ISBN 0 88760 015 8
Soft   Cover Edition ISBN 0 88760 016 6

Second Printing 1972

Third Printing 1972

Fourth Printing 1973

Published by Griffin Press Limited,
455 King Street West, Toronto 135, Canada

Printed and bound in Canada by
The Alger Press Limited

Contents

Preface

I came to the little village of Trosly-Breuil in France in 1964. There I met men who had been wounded in their minds and in their psyches when they were young. It was there that I felt called to open up a small home for other men like them . . . and so it was that the adventure of l'Arche began.

Living with Raphael and Philippe and many others who have become my brothers and sisters, I began to understand a little better the message of Jesus and his particular love for the poor in spirit and for the impoverished and weak ones of our society. I have learned much from them and feel deeply indebted to them. They have shown me what it is to live simply, to love tenderly, to speak in truth, to pardon, to receive openly, to be humble in weakness, to be confident in difficulties, and to accept handicaps and hardships with love. And, in a mysterious way, in their love they have revealed Jesus to me.

I had met Jesus before. He had called me from a career in the navy to a life of prayer and metaphysics, a life also where I loved living simply and poorly, available to the Spirit. But, it was only when I came to l'Arche that I really met and lived with men who were despised and rejected. It is there that I discovered also in a new way all those barriers in myself which cause me to despise and to reject others who are of different ways and opinions.

It was there that I discovered the two worlds that exist side by side: the world of the "normal" people, who seek social status and are motivated by ambitions of efficiency and riches, and the "abnormal" world of the despised, the handicapped, the "not-adapted-ones", be they prisoners, prostitutes, or mentally sick.

I began to see the deep wounds caused by the lack of compassion of the "normal" and "good" people; I began to sense the fear that seemed to motivate them.

And then I went to India where with some friends we were able to start up a small home for handicapped people. There I discovered the beauty, the grandure, the nobility and the simplicity of the Indian culture. Of course, I also saw much poverty. But maybe I was more struck by the interior poverty in the west. When I returned to Europe I felt deeply the squandering of riches, the hardness of hearts and the egotistical materialism of so many of the "developed" countries.

Whilst in India, I learned to love Ghandiji[1], feeling that he is one of the great prophets of our times. His deep love for the under-privileged, especially the untouchables; his desire to identify him-

---

[1] Gandhi

self with them; his openness to the spirit of God in order to become an instrument of His Peace; his desire to unite men, particularly those of opposed religions; his universal heart; his deep desire to bring peace into the world; his vision of poverty and riches; his own poverty; all these attracted me deeply. Gandhiji seemed to follow so authentically the Sermon of the Mount and the Beatitudes; those beatitudes which seem to have been for him in many ways a guiding light. Far from separating me from Jesus, Gandhiji seemed to bring me closer to Him, teaching me much about His gentleness and His tenderness. The Beatitudes of the meek seems to be none other than the deep strength, the peace, the patience and unceasing goodness and love of non-violence, "ahimsa" about which Gandhiji spoke so often. Gandhiji taught me to love Jesus more and gave me a desire to make my life more like His, especially in this domain of a struggle for peace and universal brotherhood. And this struggle can only be won by using the means of the Spirit: those of love, of gift of self, of gentleness, with no aggression or violence.

The talks that follow were written in this context. The Spirit changed my vision of the world, helped me to discover more and more the terrible divisions in our society: those which I have spoken of and those that exist between the self-satisfied civilizations of the West and the countries of Asia, Africa and South America.

How can men continue to see these divisions and inequalities without doing something drastic about them?

Never before has the world been in such need of finding men and women to follow Jesus. We must find prophets of peace who will follow in His footsteps, and who walk gently but firmly between the two worlds, calling unceasingly to the rich to dispossess themselves to find love, and calling forth to help those in suffering, misery, and poverty.

Maybe the young people, those who reject the values of our society and seek greater compassion in human relationships, will have the courage to take drastic steps, leaving the culture of ambitions and riches for the culture of the Beatitudes. May God call forth many of these to a new form of courage where they will identify themselves with the impoverished and thus bring forth a new hope for the world.

These few pages are dedicated to my brothers and sisters of l'Arche throughout the world. May I continue to walk with them on the paths of community and peacemaking until we are all gathered together in the Eternal Feast of Divine Love. Then at last there will be no more segregation and suffering, no more division and hatred, no more violence and materialism, only the quiet meeting of the spirit in the marvelous embrace that will unite us in this vast and glorious eruption of peace.

The Evolution of the Family and The Modern Crisis

I am deeply moved to be with you this evening under the auspices of this Institute of the Family, founded through the inspiration of my parents while at Rideau Hall. I hope I will not disappoint you. I have not in fact had much experience with that which pertains to the family. I had a very happy family life, thanks to wonderful parents, but am not married myself. In philosophy, I did not work particularly on the family question. So, my competence, limited in this domain, is simply that of a man who ardently desires the evolution of our society and who wishes to remain in contact with youth, and who has the joy of living in a milieu a little outside of society, in contact with those who are called "marginal people".

Since I am, in many aspects, separated from society and do not have the possibility of following the latest sociological and psychological studies, you may perhaps find me overly poetic and idealistic, far from the reality of life. However, being somewhat apart from it, do I not have the advantage of being better able to perceive some of the undercurrents controlling our existence? In any case, fully realizing my inadequacy for the task you have asked of me, I shall try very simply to express my fears and at the same time my hopes for the modern family.

I would like to sketch some of the major problems confronting today's family, which in many ways is so rich and yet so confused, motivated by an immense hope yet overwhelmed by an engulfing despair. I would like to try to discover what fundamental attitudes should be suggested in face of the present crisis, so powerful that it gives the impression of submerging everything, the true as well as the false values.

First we will see how to-day's crisis has developed with the evolution of society towards the primacy of technical and economic

1

values and the despair that followed. Next, we shall study the evolution of the family from the rural community to the small unit reduced to parents and their children. In conclusion, we shall see what ideal can be proposed to young couples.

This Institute is doomed to certain death if we make of it an Institute in defense of traditional family values. I do not need to tell you that the moment we assume a defensive attitude, we are on the road to dissolution and death. On the level of ideas, of ideologies and of life, the best defence is the propagation of truths which attract, which inflame the heart, which give birth to hope and which inspire men of good will to vital and dynamic action.

CHARACTERISTICS OF THE PRESENT CRISIS

Ten years ago, at Fribourg, I spoke on the crisis of the modern world. Since then, this crisis has evolved and spread: the upheaval in France in May, 1968; the student movements the world over; the attitudes of those called "drop-outs" who are leaving schools, colleges and universities to lead a life without norms or social convention, all oblige us to regard the crisis as a very serious reality. It is made even more so since so many of the men and women involved in these movements, reflect seriously on their actions and their consequences and are motivated by a real ideal of generosity and community living and are equally inspired by a profound sense of the value of the human person.

We could ask ourselves whether or not in 1975 our schools will be deserted because of the mass refusal to accept the system of education such as it is today. Will our streets be filled with youths who are slaves to drugs and sex? Training centres for spiritual leaders receive fewer and fewer candidates, so much so that several huge buildings, full ten years ago, are now almost empty. In the 15 years to come will we find the same void in military training centres and in schools of commerce and of the various professions which are vital to society?

Modern man thirsts for liberty. He is even drunk with liberty. And he may be destroyed by his own liberty.

Formerly, man's life and thought followed the lines of tradition and convention, but gradually, by a slow evolution in all fields, he has discovered human and artificial sources of energy which exhilarate and at the same time frighten him. The world of nature tends to be replaced by an artificial world which gives him a sense of power. Man no longer feels dominated by nature nor even obliged to serve it. On the contrary, he feels he is master of nature and that there is no longer any limit to his power.

2

The heart of man has an insatiable thirst for the unlimited and the infinite, and he is easily stifled by the chains of habit. He needs the magic of the new and the unknown. These thirsts incite him to continually change and progress and experiment in all domains.

Consider the history of man, throughout the centuries: man born in poverty, dominated by the forces of nature, evolving into man capable of walking on the moon, of unleashing nuclear energies and of continually discovering more about God's plan for matter, for man, and for the universe.

Man, as I have just said, thirsts for liberty, for freedom to live without external coercion, but above all for that internal freedom in which the forces of love, intelligence, and life can flower.

Moral and religious traditions should have led to this interior freedom from the chains of egotistic inst:ncts, social conventions, and unjust authority. Alas, too often they have stifled personal liberty instead of giving birth to it. They did not then serve the development of personal conscience but served instead a privileged group who wanted to maintain power. Instead of breaking down barriers in the heart of man and between men, these traditions created new ones.

Many men today have become conscious of the fact that frequently human and social traditions crush the individual. In the name of tradition whites have been separated from blacks, Christians from non-Christians, Jews from Arabs, the mentally unbalanced and subnormal from the normal, and the divorced from the happily married. In the name of social tradition grave injustices have been committed. In the name of law, wars have been waged. A world of hypocrisy has often been created which speaks of social values while destroying the individual. Man in applying the law has abused the poor and defenseless and in so doing he believed himself to be just! Today's youth, motivated by aspirations for freedom and the celebration of life and in the face of injustice and hypocrisy, has lost faith in tradition, social convention and authority in general. But, while rejecting what is tyrannical, arbitrary, arrogant and false in authority and tradition, he rejects also the true traditions which make up the heritage of humanity, which lead us towards the eternal, toward internal freedom and universal love.

Of course, I am not referring here only to the young who revolt against law and order simply to enjoy their own liberty. This has always occurred. I am referring to something deeper which is at the core of the present crisis. It is clear that this crisis arises from the fact that if our civilization is based partly on a Judeo-Christian tradition which ought to lead to the freedom of love, it is also partly

3

motivated by false values that are essentially materialistic and individualistic. Very often in the name of the prophets of the Jewish tradition and in the name of Jesus Christ, we have done just the opposite of what they asked. "Race of hypocrites" — these words are applicable to all of us.

The Judeo-Christian tradition represents the most fundamental and substantial heritage of humanity. It is the patrimony of past ages which orientates towards freedom of spirit. This tradition has indeed said: (Matthew 5: 2-12)

> Woe unto you who are rich, and who possess all you need,
>   and who close yourselves up in your wealth . . .
>
> Woe unto you who laugh now and who think only
>   of your possessions and your stomach . . .
>
> Blessed are you the poor . . .
>
> Blessed are you who pardon your enemies . . .
>
> Blessed are you who hunger and thirst for justice . . .
>
> Blessed are you who refuse social distinctions
>   and who regard all men as brothers . . .
>
> Blessed are you who love . . .
>
> Blessed are you who take the less fortunate into your homes
>   and hearts and who see, beyond the wrong-doer,
>   the person loved by God . . .

but we have turned our hearts and spirits away from it!

The absolute primacy of the person over social convention has too often been crushed by the primacy of law and convention which favours those in power.

The distance between the democratic and spiritual aspirations which lie at the base of our western society and the social prejudices, which too often motivate it, makes this crisis deep and leaves many minds in utter confusion. Because of these prejudices, we have taken as our supreme values efficiency and the seeking of money and comfort. Love of beauty, culture, ease, benefits of a decent life, a beautiful home, good education and social conventions have been placed above the love of the poor and the dignity of each human person. The essential, namely, the deepening of the personal conscience in freedom, life and love, has been forgotten in order to nourish an egotistic and materialistic culture.

Youth as never before has found itself torn between a choice of two aspirations: universal love, or the seeking of material gains without respect for our neighbour which engenders a hardening of the heart.

4

Means of communication, travel, and information today are such that we are all only too aware of the dramas of human existence: war and famine, people living in misery; but also of the cultural, religious and moral values of other peoples. Formerly, the impossibility of dialogue and communication between peoples excused their ignorance of one another. They could live apart, create barriers and defences against another group, and remain in utter ignorance of the positive values of traditions other than their own. The Catholic was saved and the Protestant condemned or vice versa; the Jews were the only chosen people or just the opposite, rejected by everyone. There was a clear line of demarcation between the true and the false. Our categories of people tended to be absolute.

This absolute has disappeared.

We have discovered (but perhaps not quite enough) that profound aspirations towards goodness and justice can be found in the heart of a Russian or Czech communist, and that the Christian and Jew of the western world can be dominated by a selfish desire for power and glory. Sometimes the spiritual richness and sensitivity of blacks has revealed itself in contrast to the hypocrisy and intolerance of the whites.

This coming together of peoples has broken down dogmatic thought and has incited men to believe only in the relativity of truth. A profound dislike of tradition and authority is manifested. The disappearance of traditions and of confidence in authority has caused deep disorientations in the human person and has unleashed in him aggressive and anarchistic forces which until now were controlled. Thus, there have arisen outbursts of violence, hatred, and materialism, with complete incapacity to assume responsibility, leading to a total neglect of duty and to anguish and disorder. But in face of this disappearance of social tradition, others are thirsting for authenticity and truth, and have begun to discover the real value of the human person and the sense of universal love. It seems to me that as never before in the course of history, many men, particularly amongst the young, are becoming aware of the value of the human person, irrespective of his race, religion and social standing.

At the same time, however, the necessity for economic change in our countries has led us to conceive laws and accept traditions often at the expense of the individual person. Just when many are becoming conscious of the fundamental heritage of the Judeo-Christian tradition to respect each human person, friend or foe, rich or poor, they are realizing at the same time the impossibility within the actual structure of our society to apply this truth. The very efficiency demanded by our technocratic industrial society

5

renders the life of the old, the unstable and the handicapped almost impossible. As the values of efficiency, individualism, and wealth become the only motivations, they tend to stifle the profound aspiration of man so that little by little he loses all sense of fellowship and community.

If we wish to consider the place of the family in our society as well as an ideal to propose to young people, we must understand the confusion of our youth today, and also its search for an ideal. If we do not do so, we run the risk of upholding as a model, a family closed to social values. This well-to-do family, cultivated, correct, and benevolent, with good manners, full of good will, at times produces professional men with altruistic qualities and charitable well-disposed ladies. This model has perhaps something noble about it but is inadequate today. It must be admitted that this model has often been based on a division of humanity between the wealthy and the workers, the whites and the blacks, the cultivated and the ignorant. Too often, there has been terrible pride, strong pharisaism and intolerant racism.

Allow me to quote an example from a prayer found in a prayer-book in a certain European country: "My God, teach the rich poverty in spirit and the workers the acceptance of their trials and a spirit of sacrifice."

Before determining what could be the model of a modern family, I would like to propose two subjects for reflection: first of all, the evolution of the family from the rural and communal stage to that of the modern family unit, the couple and their children; secondly, the awakening of the possessive instinct, which develops with marriage.

THE EVOLUTION FROM THE RURAL FAMILY COMMUNITY TO THAT OF THE MODERN FAMILY UNIT

In olden times, the family was a large entity. The different members lived more or less together or at least within easy reach of one another. They helped each other considerably. The family came to the aid of the aged, and the sick. Even if the family community spirit was not entirely perfect, there was nevertheless a spirit of sharing. This is evidently an idealized view for there were often internal struggles and dissensions; but the fact remains that the family was a large unit which provided a certain security: for example, if the mother fell sick she knew she could count on her own mother or sisters-in-law for help.

The family found its unity in its natural roots and in a religious tradition which increased and deepened it. Religion strengthened the family and the family found strength in religion. The father

6

or grandfather was the patriarch, the *pater familias,* the head of the large family or chief of the clan. He was in a certain respect the representative of God. Paternal authority came from God, source of all true paternity. The father was thus an image of God. His word was law. He considered himself to be the servant of the Divinity and of tradition. The spirit which prevailed in the family was conservative, respectful of law and of the maintenance of order. There is a marvellous résumé of this in the Book of Ecclesiastics (3: 3-9):

> Whoever honours his father
>> atones for his sins,
>> and whoever glorifies his mother
>> is like one who lays up treasure.

> Whoever honours his father will be gladdened
>> by his own children,
>> and when he prays he will be heard.

> Whoever glorifies his father
>> will have a long life,
>> and whoever obeys the Lord
>> will refresh his mother;
>> he will serve his parents as his masters.

> Honour your father by word and deed,
>> that a blessing from him may come upon you.

> For a father's blessing strengthens
>> the houses of his children,
>> but a mother's curse uproots their foundations.

The world has moved from this traditional, even rural vision of the family, towards an economic view of progress and evolution. The discovery of the artificial forces of energy and the invention of the machine have brought about a radical change in the structure of society and consequently of the family. Cities are no longer simply residences for the government, judges, bishops and the army, with markets for the sale of produce from the country. They have become residential centres for the labour forces of their factories. The cities' opportunities for employment, high salaries and recreation have led to their growth and a rejection of the rural life. Thus the distinction between worker and peasant has grown with all the contempt implied in that last word.

The race to the city has contributed to the disappearance of the large family. Instead of large properties, we have now two-room dwellings. Older relatives and even sick children cannot be kept at home in apartments. A complex system of hospitals, asylums, and nursing homes has been set up for the sick and the aged.

This evolution from the family community to that of the small unit has created a real insecurity in the depths of the conscience and subconscience of the couple. In the large family the members relied upon each other; one was sure of always receiving the care and material and moral help needed. Within the small family circle, one is obliged to fend for oneself alone in all the different domains of social and domestic life. As soon as the husband or his wife fall sick, the equilibrium of the family faces collapse. Financial or material insecurity has led to a radical change regarding the place and role of the mother within the family at home. Today, in many cases, it is strictly impossible for parents to have several children unless the mother works. Leaving the home, she will have to place her child in a day nursery. The home is liable to become merely a hotel, a place of lodging and not a hearth of love. The mother working long hours, at the factory or in the office, has scarcely the strength and desire to do housework. It is necessary to find a small compact apartment where the upkeep is reduced to a minimum, but which is perhaps less given to family atmosphere: there is no garden; there is less space. One necessarily has to restrict the number of children. The parents are often too exhausted to cope with their children. The children may feel abandoned and experience a real need to integrate themselves into some youth movement or youth group, or even a gang, where they can find the fellowship that is lacking in the home.

The modification of the family structure by this state of affairs is important. The couple feels isolated, surrounded by children who cost them a great deal in many ways. Sometimes they live in harassing conditions. Work in the factory which increases nervous tension has replaced the more natural work in the fields which was perhaps more tiring physically and less remunerative. In seeking a means to reduce financial insecurity, the couple has created moral and affective insecurity. The woman is constantly in contact with other men and thus less dependent on her husband. She is in a situation where she can become deeply attached to another. The husband's insecurity can incite him to become jealous and aggressive, and the wife feeling this developing possessiveness may in turn become aggressive. The couple becomes a little universe of growing tension and latent hostility. The spirit of this new family is no longer conservative; the *pater familias* no longer exists, even the ties between parents and children are totally different. There is either a complete abdication of all authority and even of responsibility, or relations within the family may often take on a more fraternal, supple manner.

The large conservative family with its type of authority gave a certain moral, spiritual and material security. This security does not exist any more. The man and wife often experience a great poverty when confronted by each other and are incapable of establishing a true relationship of friendship. They try to drown their fear and anguish in excessive professional activity and in seeking after material wealth, hoping to make up for their lack of deep seated security by the illusory security of wealth and social ambition.

Until now I only wanted to note the development that has come about, more or less in different countries and regions. Today, the family unit, whether it likes it or not, is reduced to the couple and their children. The large family scarcely exists, and it is even difficult to maintain one's circle of friends because of the continual movement from city to city for professional reasons. With each change of residence, new bonds of friendship must be created.

The traditional people may lament the disappearance of the large family and may try in particular situations to resist these tendencies by constituting rural communities. These attempts at rural living are very laudable but it must be admitted that they run in every way contrary to the current of our society which does not favour this return to the land.

It seems to me that if our Institute is called to help the family to take its true place in modern society, it must look for the positive and dynamic elements in the aspirations of the modern family in order to help it truly progress, and not merely evolve in decadence under the appearance of progress.

THE RISE OF THE POSSESSIVE INSTINCT DURING MARRIED LIFE

I would like to go on to the second point, to consider the birth of the possessive instinct at the moment of the foundation of a family. I have often been struck by the transformation which reveals itself in the hearts and spirits of the newly-weds. Before marriage, the young man was full of ideals and often acted idealistically. He was ready to struggle in poverty for social justice or for the propagation of philosophical, political or religious ideas. He could live under difficult conditions. He was generous with his time and possessions. In this spirit, he meets a young girl inspired by the same ideals and they decide to work together. They marry and very quickly they start to install themselves, seeking greater comfort. Their life begins to change radically. Little by little the ideals which had motivated the couple disappear. They tend gradually to close themselves up upon each other and their children. They seek a comfortable family life. If they go out, it is for professional or social reasons. They become imprisoned by their possessions, their way of life and social class, they lose that taste for adventure and that thirst for justice which formerly inspired them. They forget that not very far away, there are grave injustices, the poor, the unfortunate, and the handicapped for whose welfare they had struggled before marriage.

The birth of a child in a family is too often the occasion for withdrawal into its own little world. It should be above all the moment when parents look towards more universal horizons. The appearance of this new person who is free and cannot be led around as one might wish is a true mystery: a mystery which should bring a new depth to the couple and a new gift to the universe. The child does not belong to the parents; he is not their possession, but rather he has been confided to them in order that he may serve man, his brother. The birth of a child should constitute a new period in the life of the couple. The child itself represents a risk for his parents. Where will he take them? Indeed the parents are not there to form the child according to their own image but to help him find his true self and to become truly free in relation to his instincts and to his milieu in order that he may love better. Is this instinct for possession and this search for comfort, which reveal themselves especially with the birth of the child, a sort of defence in relation to this pressing call which appears at the same moment, namely the call to receive the gift of God which is the child and to be more open to God and to men?

THE IDEAL

It is easy in our time to be swallowed up in the stagnant waters of our society which constantly encourage us to look out for ourselves. It is difficult to go against the current social life which urges us to acquire wealth and look for material well-being. Should we not strongly condemn the system of commercial propaganda through radio, television and magazines? It only accentuates the deep insecurity in the heart of the young. A society which accepts or is prone to accept this deceit, whose sole object is the expansion of trade and not the welfare of the consumers, is surely on the road to the most serious degeneration. To struggle for the family is meaningless if we do not resist this deceitful publicity. This publicity leads men continually to live in frustration, for one can never possess everything. The publicity to which they are exposed at every instant, prevents men from opening up to essential values that lead them to commune with each other. And, to think that in our country, the means of communication which mould the minds and hearts of men are in the hands of big business which finances them!

In this situation, what ideal can we propose to young couples? As I just said, we must make every effort to resist the propaganda presented by the mass media which continually incites men to work for material acquisitions. It is not, however, just a matter of banning erotic literature and cheap films, but rather of proposing an ideal which attracts men and incites them to the dynamism of the gift of self. The world is so close to cataclysm that we must present a demanding ideal to the young and claim a complete gift of self which goes beyond ease and comfort.

UNION OF LOVE BETWEEN MAN AND WOMAN

Parallel to the evolution of family patterns which we have spoken of, another evolution can be discerned in the relationship between man and woman. In the ancient civilizations the woman was considered as inferior, fit only to do domestic work and to bear children. Frequently, she held a position scarcely above that of the slaves. Love between man and woman was then considered as passion without human value. True friendship could not in fact exist between man and woman as the latter, according to the ancients, did not possess the intelligence required to communicate with man and to participate in his activities. In order to find friendship, the womenfolk grouped amongst themselves, as did the men.

The idea that woman was not an inferior being but equally as important as man evolved over the centuries. This evolution took two forms. In one case, woman wished to become man, as if there were no difference between them; while, in the other case, equality was conceived as complementary. It is this second type of equality that I wish to consider.

In Genesis it is said: "God created man; He created them, man and woman." Psychologists confirm spiritual and psychological differences to be as profound as the anatomical differences that exist between man and woman. Man loves in a different manner from woman. The needs of man are different from those of woman. It is just these differences which make a vital union between them possible. In order to love, the woman needs the spiritual and physical strength of man as much as he requires her tenderness, patience, and intuition. In this union, woman is loved by man as a unique person who is complementary to him and in whom the spirit of the Infinite resides. Modern thought inspired more or less by Judeo-Christian thought sees in the relationship of love uniting man and woman not a useless passion but a secret and sacred mystery which can open each to the Infinite, not turning them away from God, but rather uniting them more closely to Him.

Here we touch upon the mystery of love. What is love, a myth or a reality? A true experience or an illusion? Is love a real goal or

11

is it an escape? It is represented in multiple ways, on television, radio and in films. It is spoken about on every street corner, in highly mystical works as well as in the most obscene pornographic magazines. It is a magic word which expresses a profound call or desire of the human heart. The word love has been so abused by publicity and advertisements that we no longer know really what it means. Is it an ephemeral attraction between man and woman which is expressed in the sex act? Is it a game, a pastime, an adventure, a desire to seduce or dominate? Or is it a human and even a divine reality, the summit of friendship implying a gift, an experience outside time and faithfulness within time?

Love is the highest and the most profound mystery of the universe, the source and end of all things, but it implies force of character, inner fidelity, intelligence, delicacy of heart and above all the capacity to listen, to accept and to place oneself at the disposition of the other. These attitudes are rare in our society but rare things are often the most beautiful and the heart and mind of man must be opened out towards them.

It is the incomparable treasure of love and of union alone that can bring happiness to man.

The human person can never really accept the limits of his earthly condition. Continually he seeks to break through the bars which imprison him within himself as he stretches forth towards the universal. He tries to attain the infinite through knowledge, through the conquest of space and nuclear discoveries, artistic creativity or the treacherous experience of drugs and even violence; but above all, it is attained through the oblatory experience of real love, through a love which is receptive, which is communion, gift, and pardon; for the very nature of the Infinite which is God, is Love. The richness of love gratifies all the unrest and seeking of the human heart and spirit. Compensations in material wealth and semblances of the infinite are sought after when one does not rest in the Infinite. He who loves can remain poor. Men of our day desire, wish and aspire for this treasure of true love. But alas, they often lack the moral fibre to acquire it. They despair on the way and become closed within themselves, or else surrender to sexual play which has nothing dynamic or deeply satisfying about it.

In ancient times, because of social tradition and the context of the large joint family, husband and wife scarcely met on a personal level. They could live together in an atmosphere of indifference, made up of neither love nor hate. They could live under the same roof, supported or hidden by the tribe.

Today as never before man and woman find themselves face to face. They must meet each other as persons, not simply as instruments of procreation or members of society. They must discover each other as husband and wife and live together a deep union, that of two free persons merging into one. This fusion does not take place without difficulty or hardship or the renunciation of egocentricity and human meanness. In order to really meet, the spouses must divest themselves of all impurities of selfishness in order to find the limpidity and freedom of love which implies a work of daily fidelity to one another, to truth and to the Spirit of God. In order to really love, they must learn in the school of time and trials; true love is at the summit of a long road, the road of life. If this meeting does not take place, husband and wife, after a certain temporary period of happiness, can become aggressive and consider the other partner as infringing on his liberty by his very presence.

We can say that, presently, the family is at a crossroad: we are either entering into a new era of union between man and woman, a deeper union resulting from the meeting of two mysteries, or we are moving towards a catastrophe and to the disappearance of the family as a human reality. Perhaps our society is moving towards a life of promiscuity, of sexual orgies similar to those referred to in the decadent periods of the Roman Empire and of the Greek civilization. Perhaps in seeking only for sexual harmony, one will consider the constant changing of bed companions as normal . . . "provided there is love". The profound value of chastity and of faithfulness in times of hardship will be disregarded. We will have forgotten the importance of that love which unites old people, love still as fresh and as young as on the day of their engagement. Children will suffer all the consequences of having many so-called mothers and fathers. For the child, in order to have healthy physical, moral and psychic development, needs the nourishment of the united love of his parents. If our society loses the concept of family life and falls into moral decadence, then we must be prepared to enter into an age of tension and violence, fruits of deep anguish. I have personally too frequently encountered the anxiety and aggressivity of children and adults who have come from disturbed family situations. In the degree that unfaithfulness in love increases we can be sure that the number of anguished children and adults will increase. Then, the world will gradually turn into a jungle, moved for the most part by the forces of hate and destruction.

When confronted with great personal and social difficulties, as in all critical times, man will either give way to despair or else deep and unsuspected strength will be called forth from within him to meet the situation.

I am convinced that in the present time, in spite of the difficulties man has to meet another in a state of oblation, communion and gift of self, there are latent hidden forces in him which can be awakened in order to enable him to discover and live this reality of love and fidelity. In order to really penetrate into this mystery of the union of the couple, it is essential that each one acquire an interior maturity, a maturity that is perhaps rare. I would add that in order to be truly united and to remain truly faithful to one another, the couple must listen and be open to the Spirit of God who has reserved for Himself the science of the heart. The heart of man is satisfied only by the Infinite and to discover this Infinite in union he must open himself to the Spirit of God, a spirit of giving, of receiving. The union between the two spouses can thus deepen to such an extent that they enter in a mystical manner into the very life of God Himself.

Even in spite of the frailty and ephemeral quality in the love of a newly engaged couple, there is something poetic, liberating, exhilarating and ecstatic about it. It detaches them in some way from this everyday world and they experience new happiness. But this love experienced by a young engaged couple is but a poor reflection of divine love, but an inkling of its full mystery. It gives but a short-lived and partly imaginary happiness. Love which flows from the Infinite can have the same characteristics of exaltation; but a note of seriousness and realism is added — the seriousness of commitment and of total giving of self to the limits of one's strength, as well as an opening of the heart to all men, and particularly to those who are suffering or in misery. This new love which unites the modern family is a real fusion which unites them even to God. A current of divine life flows from one to the other and each is revealed to the other as an aspect of the Infinite, each discovers in the other the presence of God — the eternal presence so desired by man in every epoch, and particularly by men of our nuclear age. What certain people seek in the experience of art and creativity, or in the often illusory hopes of science, or the exhilarating experiments with drugs and sex, the couple, moved by the Spirit of God, finds in the love which unites them, a love which is as romantic and poetic as the great loves of humanity, as realistic, as total and as sacrificial as those of the prophets and the mystics.

Flowing from this union, source of a plenitude of joy, the love of the couple reveals itself through the daily acceptance of the limits and faults of each other and in mutual openness. It is this acceptance in and through gentleness, kindness, forgiveness, confidence and the desire to see shining in the other the warm light of the Spirit of God that becomes the great sign of the merciful love of God for man and of His incessant forgiveness.

14

Contrary to the love which encloses the two spouses and their children upon themselves, this new love is completely open to others, and especially to the poor. The outburst of the energy of love all too often encloses the couple in an illusory world, a soap bubble reflecting a thousand colours of the most marvellous shades but which bursts and evaporates once in contact with the harsh realities of life. Above all, this illusory world disintegrates with the discovery of the real personality of the other which is often poor and close to despair and anguish or proud, jealous, touchy and fearful.

Modern man calls out for a love which brings deep happiness to the two concerned but at the same time overflows with force and gentleness upon others — first on their own children and then on all the poor and unfortunate. The first flow of this love is certainly onto their own children, in their readiness to receive, and raise them. Our world needs a large number of generous men and these will only be the fruits of parents who are united and motivated by a great ideal.

The mystery which is felt in the heart of the partner through union with him opens one up to a sentiment of universal love and of compassion for all those who suffer on this earth. The more one discovers the person, his capacities, and the sense of the infinite in him, the more this sense of the human person becomes acute. Thus, as the union between the spouses deepens, the more they fuse into one, the more they are able to offer themselves together with their children, to all men and especially to the less fortunate. Their united hearts become a source of love and strength for those who need them. Together then they seek to realize the desire of Charles de Foucauld, the hermit of the Sahara, to become a universal brother.

Love which encloses and constructs barriers is not true love. It is perhaps a stage of immaturity. If the lovers will not advance from the beginning towards sacrifice and common gift of self to others, to their neighbour and to the less fortunate, they lack something; and this will be manifested later in tensions, degenerating into jealousy or hatred, apathy or even despair.

For man and woman to really discover each other, their union must be based on an ideal which orients them towards a better world. These ecstatic demands of love will have important repercussions on the possessive instinct to which I have already referred.

Such new couples will not be closed in on themselves. On the contrary, their moments of intimacy should open them to those neighbours who are rejected or abandoned — the depressed, the

15

aged, and the handicapped. They will receive into their homes those who are hungry for food and affection, and they will be ready to render service, visit the sick, help the miserable. Their doors, signs of their hearts, will always be open. Instead of structuring their lives on the acquisition of material wealth, they will structure them on openness to others.

Those who cannot receive the unfortunate into their homes will be open to activities of service. Their lives will then be completely absorbed in their gift of self to the less fortunate.

Others will even be called to leave their own milieu. The love which unites them and flows out to their children and to others, will incite them not just to give the excess of their wealth to the poor, or to give of their professional capacities, but to give much more — the gift of their person. Thus, they will live with their children in poor areas of their own country, or in developing countries. By assuming a role among the less fortunate they will discover different modes of life: some will be there just to be open to the numerous situations and activities which may present themselves, to advise, support, encourage, and comfort the needy; some will practise their profession in the metropolis, returning to their simple and hospitable homes in the evenings; still others will open dispensaries or work in these areas as teachers, nurses, social workers, doctors or lawyers — all at the service of the poor, and receiving little or no remuneration. Still others will establish homes as centres of prayer, as witnesses to the Invisible.

Certainly, this new life demands a confidence that is particularly audacious. The maternal instinct gives the mother a strong desire to protect her children and to refuse all contact with a world that is less healthy and that could introduce them to disease and harmful habits of life. Normally, the father wishes that his eldest son bear the name that he himself received, and that his son acquire a social standing. He can only accept living otherwise if he discovers that his action, their action, can help transform society precisely through example, tenacity and non-violent perseverance. The children will not suffer. Of course, several worthy people will advise against such a life of hardship for children. But a child suffers only in an atmosphere of tension when the vital union between the parents is lacking. If, on the contrary, the parents are happy in their life of service to others, and if their union deepens, we can be sure that the children conceived by their union will grow in all aspects, nourished by the unselfish lives of their parents founded in joy and in poverty.

This ideal for a family is only possible however, if it is lived in union with other families. Moments of discouragement will be overcome by such a union with others. The couples will not necessarily live all together, but the same current of life will pass through them all. They will be inspired by the same desire for justice and truth, the same wish to be present to the needs of the poor. This large community of couples and friends will be a source of hope and strength, an undercurrent bringing warmth and light in a society overcome by despair.

CONCLUSION

Facing the seriousness of the present crisis, we should not be afraid to present a high ideal implying love and self-giving. The days of the lord of the manor, of benevolent and charitable ladies and welfare committees organizing fairs and sales for the poor are over, even if they were bearers of authentic values in their time. I would even say that the extreme devotion of professional men — doctors, lawyers, government officials, professors, teachers, social workers — but who seek at the same time to augment their material wealth, and to live comfortably, is insufficient today. The crisis is now much more profound and serious. To meet it, we must follow our logic to its ultimate end. The gift of oneself to others can no longer be simply on the level of giving "spare time" during leisure hours or on a professional level. It must be on a deeper, more personal level.

You will say to me: "What you are proposing as an ideal family is not possible, is unrealistic." I will answer by asking you some questions: Do you really think, looking clearly at the facts, that our society can continue as it is now without committing collective suicide? Do you not realize that the grave injustices in the slums of South Amercia, in the large cities of Europe and Asia, the injustices committed against the negroes in the United States and in Africa, the injustices throughout the world, are smoldering fires that may burst into flames in the near future? Do you not see that there are tremendous powers ready to unite the discontented and to stimulate the revolutionaries? Do you really believe that the world tensions: U.S.-Russia, Russia-China, China-U.S., Eastern countries-Russia, Israel-Arabs, North and South Vietnam, etc., will not explode one day into a devastating fire and that we will not use the nuclear arms that science has put at our disposition? Do you really think that the inactivity of youth, their lack of ideal and the absence of motivation are not going to lead our society to despair? Do you not think that the terrible waste in the West in front of the penury and misery in other countries is going to arouse an aggressiveness that will overflow one day? Do you really think that we can continue with our compromising religions which make no real demands on our persons, with our system of middle-class, "do-gooder" morality,

17

with our luxurious neighbourhoods, and large homes, and all of this next door to the slums and unending misery? Do you really think we can continue to propagate, through advertisements and propaganda, a morality of egotistic and materialistic pleasure when in reality, more than ever before, we need generosity and an ideal?

I am certain that this state of affairs cannot continue. Our society will be transformed through the fire of revolution or through the stagnant waters of decadence or through the fire and peace of true love. There is still time. But time is short. To confront the seriousness of this crisis and in face of these grave injustices, a new race of men and women capable of great generosity is required. I see this generosity in the eyes of youth. They are our hope. It is they who can bring us radical solutions. It is they who will have the courage to take the decisive steps to remedy the injustices of the past, not by the path of vociferous or revolutionary criticism but through an active and massive non-violent approach. The ideal of the family of our epoch must correspond to the gravity of the present day crisis. For society to convert itself, or rather for men of today to turn away from materialistic egoism and from violence and revolution, the married couples of today must burn with new hearts and new spirits — hearts of flesh and spirits of fire as spoken of by the prophet Ezekiel (36: 25-27).

> I will sprinkle clean water upon you, and you
>   shall be cleaned from all your uncleannesses,
>   and from all your idols I will cleanse you.
>
> A new heart I will give you and a new spirit I will
>   put within you;
>
> And I will take out of your flesh the heart of stone
>   and give you a heart of flesh.
>
> And I will put my spirit within you . . .

There must be a more authentic receptivity and openness, a more radical poverty, greater hope and audacity, and a keener thirst for justice and truth. A new generation of men and women is needed who have complete confidence in the action of the Spirit of God and who will leave the security of the extended family, of wealth and material welfare in order to live in the hands of God so that they may spread the spirit of truth, peace and love in their own countries or in others where misery is more blatant.

The extended family dominated by tradition and the *pater familias* served its purpose in its day, but now the evil is too great, the decadence is too acute, and above all, the possibilities of hatred, revolution and death are so widespread that this ideal of the family no longer suffices. United couples, burning with love for humanity, poor as St. Francis and willing to spread this ideal of peace are required. More than ever we need men as great in the domain of love as the astronauts and the great scientists of to-day.

In conclusion, allow me to give some more practical suggestions, for time is short and we have to be ready to face new situations.

Family associations, trained medical helpers, social workers: stay open to new formulas. Do not scorn young people full of generosity and ideals but who lack sometimes the technical know-how. They will be the originators of these new formulas. Your technical capacity must be completed by their dynamism, their openness and their hope. The less fortunate, in order to regain a taste for living, must find people who are willing to share their lives and who communicate a truly human motivation. It is these young couples who can bring the indispensable complementary element of love which engenders hope. Do not forget that these young people so full of idealism need your technical knowledge and your experience. We must know how to co-operate together, each in his place, each with his specific role.

Religious and spiritual leaders: proclaim without fear that God loves each one of us, each human person and thirsts to communicate His Holy Spirit. Proclaim this Spirit promised by Isaiah, Jeremiah, Ezekiel, Joel and Jesus Christ, and be vigilant in encouraging those who receive Him and who want to walk with Him. Encourage and give support to the young couples who choose this new form of life. Give them the young priests, ministers, spiritual leaders that they need to advise them and to maintain the fire in their hearts.

Parents: you may be disconcerted by the new formulas of the young. But, have confidence. Encourage them; do not restrain them. Do not stifle, through money and comfort, the development of the germs of life in them and of an ideal. Let them blossom out in these new forms of poverty. Accept their generosity which is different from yours. Times have changed. Needs are different. Do not overly protect your grandchildren and do not be afraid for them. It is the authenticity of the ideal, and the generosity of the heart and purity of intention which counts before God. In encouraging them, you will participate in the activity of your children. You will draw blessings upon yourselves and you will discover very quickly that a deep friendship will be established between you and your children. The generation gap will disappear. There will no longer be social classes or racial struggles, we hope, but only brothers and sisters in the eyes of the same Father working to establish justice and peace in the world.

You, young people, young couples, couples of all ages, who are ready to hear the call, go forward. Follow your conscience. Let your spirits and hearts speak. Do not restrain, or sadden the Spirit. With courage, break through the structures of the past, open your hearts wide to the Spirit of God which is the spirit of welcome and giving, and know that God loves and helps those who follow His Spirit and who live for the unfortunate and who assume real and permanent responsibilities on their behalf. You may have moments of great discouragement, particularly when pressures weigh upon you in order to make you let go. Hold firm to your decision. Your work, often obscure and unrewarding, is the seed which will bring forth the new society of brotherhood, justice and peace. Listen to Yahveh speaking to us through the mouth of Isaiah (58: 6-12):

> Is not this the fast that I choose:
> to loose the bonds of wickedness,
> to undo the thongs of the yoke,
> to let the oppressed go free,
> and to break every yoke?

> Is it not to share your bread with the hungry,
> and bring the homeless poor into your house
> when you see the naked to cover him
> and not to hide yourself from your own flesh?

> Then your light shall break forth like the dawn,
> and your healing shall spring up speedily;

> Your righteousness shall go before you;
> the glory of the Lord shall be your rear guard.

> And the Lord will guide you continually
> and satisfy your desire with good things,
> and make your bones strong,
> and you shall be like a watered garden,
> like a spring of water,
> whose waters never fail.

> And your ancient ruins shall be rebuilt;
> you shall raise up the foundations of many
> generations,
> you shall be called the repairer of the breach,
> the restorer of streets to dwell in.

Faced with the breaches which appear in our society, is this not our hope?

Love Presence and Communion

The world of presence and communion is an integral part of our being. It is also a subject so vast and engulfing that is difficult here to give anything but a brief introduction.

There are several aspirations of the human being. The first, which we have felt ourselves or in the boys and girls or the adults for whom we are responsible, is *the need to live*. This need is translated by a thirst for liberty and independence, by a desire to progress, evolve, create and do beautiful things. It is felt also in the need to orientate one's life towards the universal truths, to accomplish what is noble and generous and to be recognized by others for what we have done. One of the greatest sufferings of man is to feel imprisoned, limited. Man is constantly seeking to break through the limits of his being; he refuses to be closed in. That is why our hearts are often filled when we are before vast horizons and mountains. These needs for life, action and creation are part of an *aspiration towards light*. . . . which attracts us; we like to look at it, to be warmed by it, and to rest in its harmony and beauty.

But still deeper, there is a thirst in the heart of man, a deep yearning *to be understood,* to be loved and to love. I need someone near me with whom I can share, with whom I can feel secure. I can relax in and with him. If I am alone, I may feel lonely, even anguished. And we know what can result from this anguish: we may harden our hearts in order to erase or smother it; or we may simply refuse to live. This is the feeling of those who feel rejected; who believe they have no place in the universe. These sentiments are in each one of us at one time or another . . . . to feel not wanted, useless, without any value. This impression of solitude is expressed very simply by Prévert[1] in one of his poems. He reminds us how

---

[1] "Early Breakfast" Jacques Prévert translated by William E. Baker, Twayne Publishers, Inc., New York, 1967.

much we need the look of a friend who says: "I love you very much. I believe you have an important place in the universe and most especially for me, in my heart."

He put coffee
In the cup
He put cream
In the cup of coffee
He put sugar
In the coffee cup
With the little spoon
He stirred it up
He tried a sip
He put back the cup
He never spoke
He lit
A cigarette
He made rings
Of the smoke
He put the ashes
In the ash tray
Without talking to me
Without taking note
He stood up
He put
His hat on his head
He put on his raincoat
Because it was a rainy day
And he went away
Without a word
Without a glance aside
And me I laid
My head in my hand
And I cried[1]

Who has not known this pain? "He left without even looking at me"? Or perhaps we have aroused this feeling in others: we did

---

[1]*Ibid.*

not look at them as we should have, with the love that they deserved, and they cried. Oh! Perhaps the tears were invisible tears of silence and non-life, or perhaps tears of aggression and violence.

These aspirations of the human being towards life, light and love are intermingled. I will speak mainly of the latter, the thirst for communion and communication, the need to be looked at, understood, loved and to love.

Here I would like to note some of the aspirations which are linked to this need for communication and communion. To begin with, we find the *need to express ourselves.* As the flower spreads her perfume and the sun the warmth of its rays, we need to radiate through our words and actions. The gift of words is wonderful but it has no meaning in itself. Its value is only in the degree it comes from the heart of one person and enters into the heart of another, bringing forth new life.

I will not go too much into this domain of the spoken word and what it can do to bring life or death. We know that in order to speak there must be someone to listen. By that listening alone there is already a sharing. (Although there are several ways of listening. We can listen with so many defense mechanisms that we do not truly receive the other, or we can listen with love.)

Man needs to express himself and in many different ways: through words, acts, creative imagination, procreation and many more. He needs to share his possessions and his person. It is fundamental to his being and if he does not find a friend with whom he can share he may fall into a world of sadness and even violence.

There is likewise a deep aspiration in man towards *simplicity* and *poverty.* We desire to do away with the barriers separating us so that with simplicity and joy we may truly speak and express our inner feelings and live in communion with others. We want to have the feeling of life circulating freely and fully from one to the other. We want to escape the hypocrisy and falsehood which keep us from simplicity in our relationships. This feeling is sometimes very real in community life. And we all work more or less in communities. How we long for more true simplicity in our friendships!

There is also in the human heart a deep *thirst for risk.* All of us have this thirst, and the day we no longer take risks something will have died in us. In friendship there is this risk. I discover in the other a free person and by that very fact, as a psychologist said, a "dangerous" person. He is dangerous to me because, in the end, I can never know him completely. He may hurt me. There is a mystery in him — the mystery of his liberty. I must respect him. He is free to love me and I to love him. Youth today has this taste for risk, but often fears that which follows: commitment.

Another need of the human being which is linked to this mystery of presence and communion is the *need for security*. When we came into this life we needed to have someone next to us; someone to feed us, wash us and love us. And we know that we will most certainly have another moment in our lives when we will live this same type of poverty. We begin our lives in great poverty and we will end them in the same poverty. If today I am able to eat alone, live alone, the day will come when I am no longer able to do so. Written in the metaphysics of my being is the metaphysics of my death. At some moment, when I am sick and dying, I will need to have someone near me, to comfort and assure me. One day I will need a friend's consolation.

Here we discover two aspects at the base of friendship: infinity in poverty and death, and infinity in exaltation and joy. They are the two poles in the life of man. Man needs to find a friend who can share his joys as well as his sufferings. He needs to have a faithful and unselfish friend who will not leave him. At the time when man touches the infinity of death he needs a compassionate presence in which he can foretaste in love something of the infinity which surpasses death. In this call to communion there is a secret call towards the infinite of which S. Nacht speaks in *The Presence of the Psychoanalyst*:

> "It is a truth well known to all of us psychoanalysts; that man is motivated by two aspirations which are fundamental and opposite: one, positive, which moves him to love, to unite and to construct; the other, negative, which moves him to hate, to separate and to destroy . . .
>
> It may happen during the course of an analysis that we touch this deeper, more secret, more immovable area of the psyche characterized by an intense need for absolute union. Here the individual seems to seek nothing more than a return to his original state where separation did not yet exist. It seems that fear, mother of all the misfortunes of man, began at the moment of this first separation and that he has kept this thirst to find once again this state of union, peace, plenitude — a preobjectal state par excellence — a profound desire to be one with the object and to be melted into him.
>
> Philosophers of all ages have recognized this fundamental need for union which is in each man, each interpreting it according to his own vision of the world, whether it be the ancient philosophy of Lao-Tse or the pre-Socratic philosophy of Heraclitus, or that of Bergson."

In the heart of man there will always be two ways of reaching out towards the infinite: either through *union* love and creation or through separation and destruction, for destruction also holds something of the infinite . . . annihilation is like an imitation, a caricature, of creation from nothing.

The Poverty and Wealth of Man Seeking Communion

We know the confusion man feels if his thirst for communion is in any way frustrated, wounded or damaged. Each of us has lived such experiences or knows another who has. If a friend with whom I feel deeply united is unfaithful or betrays me there is something broken within me. If the gift of my being, my love, is hurt, then very quickly I lose all motivation, all taste for living. I am sad. I think, for example, of the prisoners of war who, on returning home in 1945 looked for their wives and children only to find their homes deserted. They no longer wanted to live. They fell into alcoholism and the life of a tramp.

This deep weakness or vulnerability of the heart is also seen in and through the frustrations of a child who never received the love which was his right; he was and feels rejected. This is so often the case for many of the children we are responsible for. A child, born into a deeply united family, discovers his own value through the loving presence of his parents. He gains confidence in himself, discovering that he is a unique being, infinitely precious, because his parents treat him that way. He knows that everything he does, good or bad, touches the heart of his mother. If he does something good, she is happy and laughs; if he does something bad, she is unhappy. Whatever he does provokes profound emotion in the hearts of those who love him. He is not treated as an indifferent being.

But the child who has never been treated in this unique way, as infinitely mysterious and ineffable, how will he develop? He may feel rejected. He may have a deep feeling of solitude . . . loneliness. And from this anguish can be born many things . . . For when I am in this state of anguish I try to escape it by refusing life and reality. I risk falling into a serious psychosis. I refuse reality because for me reality means hatred and abandonment. There is no one who is interested in me. I feel as if I am dying and because of this I do not want this world. So I cut myself off from it. I enter into myself and find a world of dreams and hallucinations. There I feel a little more at ease in contrast to the way I feel in the exterior world of hatred, suffering, and chaos — the world that Sartre describes. We may criticize Sartre but too often what he says is true. That is the drama of our present world! There are many people who have never known the mystery of the union of two persons. The only relation they know is the relationship of abusive possession or rejection. There are children who live Sartre's words: "Hell is others".

A man, if he has never known a close true relationship with another, cannot live in harmony with others, looking peacefully at the universe, loving generosity and an ideal and all that is beautiful. He will be an anguished person, feeling frustrated. Other people, the universe, are things against which he must fight. He must dominate them, or else they will violate him. The core of his being has not been structured by the presence of someone who said, "You are precious to me. You are mysterious to me. I love you." So he leaves the exterior world to live in his world of dreams which ends in anguish, followed by despair and in an attitude of non-life or violence.

If, on the other hand, these thirsts of men are in some way quenched, then what extraordinary wealth! Others are no longer hell but paradise. With them he can establish a mysterious communion. While still completely himself, he becomes the other. Their two liberties meet in a unique kiss from which life bursts forth. The human heart, when motivated by love, is something extraordinary. Man is capable of doing the greatest and most beautiful things.

This leads me to speak of vitality and motivation. Let us think here of the daily chores of a mother. She gets up early in the morning, works long hours, day after day, simply because her child is there. She becomes dynamic because of him. The call of the child, metaphysical, physical and psychological, arouses an extraordinary amount of strength in the mother. Whenever we love, whenever there is this impulse of love in the heart, we are capable of the most marvellous acts. Love is stronger than death. When we are motivated by a cause, liberty for example, energies are born within us that give us exceptional power. It is likewise in our activities with the children and adults who are our responsibility. If we are really motivated in their service we feel the powers of creativity and dynamism rise up in us. We are happy and we communicate this joy. In contrast, if this motivation dies out, everything becomes difficult. We have lead in our feet. We watch the clock. We radiate our sadness.

Sometime ago, I read a beautiful book by Victor Frankl: *Man's Search for Meaning*. He shows us that the basic problem of man is above all that of motivation. Give someone hope, give him motivation, and you give him life. As soon as the boys and girls entrusted to us begin to take an interest in something, they become more integrated; they begin to work. If we want to go to an extreme we could ask: Does laziness really exist? Is it not rather a question of motivation?

Frankl's book is fascinating. The author was imprisoned in a concentration camp and the first section relates his experience in the camp, and describing those who survived, and those who did not, and why. It is earth-shattering! He gives some very concrete examples which show how hope was a primary factor in the lives of those who survived the suffering. To the extent that a prisoner maintained a thirst for life he found the strength to overcome difficulties. I would like to cite a passage from his book where he tells of his experience during a long forced march with other prisoners. The thought of his wife, also in a concentration camp, came to his mind.

"A thought transfixed me: for the first time in my life I saw the truth as it is set into song by so many poets, proclaimed as the final wisdom by so many thinkers. The truth — that love is the ultimate and the highest goal to which man can aspire. Then I grasped the meaning of the greatest secret that human poetry and human thought and belief have to impart: *The salvation of man is through love and in love.* I understood how a man who has nothing left in this world still may know bliss, be it only for a brief moment, in the contemplation of his beloved. In a position of utter desolation, when man cannot express himself in positive action, when his only achievement may consist in enduring his sufferings in the right way — an honourable way — in such a position man can, through loving contemplation of the image he carries of his beloved, achieve fulfillment. For the first time in my life I was able to understand the meaning of the words, "The angels are lost in perpetual contemplation of an infinite glory."[1]

Most of us know people who have lived in a certain amount of comfort and who suddenly lost everything, but they kept the essential: a friend. And, in keeping him, they kept a certain happiness. There was certainly great sorrow but their inner being, their life, was not destroyed. In suffering and in difficulty, if a friend is there, near us, if we can share, there is a wisp of wind which warms the heart. When all material goods are lost, we have not lost all, not the essential, if the friend remains.

Misery, on the other hand, is the person without a friend. "And me I laid my head in my hand and I cried . . ." The miserable per-

---

[1]Viktor E. Frankl, *Man's Search for Mean, An Introduction to Logotherapy.* Copyright 1959-1962, by Viktor E. Frankl. Reprinted by permission of Beacon Press.

son is he who, having lost all motivation, all hope, has no one. Read, if you will, the words of Job. You will discover what it is to be a miserable man when he says, "Even my children make fun of me . . . my friends, those who were most precious to me, turn their heads from me . . ." That is truly the miserable man, one who feels abandoned because he is despised, because he feels unworthy of the respect and love of another. And feeling abandoned he falls into a world of sadness, non-life and even violence.

The miserable man is he who has never heard anyone say to him: "You are my son." He has known teachers, perhaps, who loved him for a few months or even years. But after that he was changed to another institution. And there again he may have found good people but after a few more years he was changed to still another home. He has never had that anchor in life which gives security. As a result of this constant change he may think to himself: "I will be leaving this place in a few years . . . why bother getting attached to anyone here? Why bother loving anyone for I will be leaving soon . . . it's not worth it! I wonder what kind of a place I will be in next? Who will I find? I have no one! I have no security!"

As I have said before, the small child gains confidence in himself through the attention he receives from his parents. Think of the child in good health, happy, lying between his father and mother . . . the pride of his parents when they speak of him as the most beautiful baby! These things are very important for the psychic development of the child. If the mother did not believe that he was the most wonderful baby in the world, that there is no smile like his, that he has begun to walk before other babies; if she did not have that feeling of his *unique* importance, that child would not gain the confidence in himself which is absolutely necessary for his growth. Because his mother gets up when he cries he knows he is important. He needs to feel that someone cares for him, is ready to get up in the middle of the night, to leave her comfort, to sacrifice her life — just for him.

The miserable person has never felt that . . . or he no longer feels it. There is no one who would bother to get up for him. And this is the sad plight of a child we call maladjusted or retarded. If his handicap is a sword in the hearts of his parents, this sword is double-bladed in the heart of the handicapped. First of all, because he is handicapped; secondly, because he feels the pain he causes his parents, their sadness and anguish. This is transmitted to him through the constant and anguished steps taken to find a doctor who might help . . . then the deep disappointment . . . and still more disappointments. And finally his parents' resignation which is perhaps worst of all. For this resignation is really a "giving up". "I must keep this child, that's the way it is." All this anxiety on the part of the parents bursts forth within the child. He feels their sadness. He feels he is of no value.

I have often had the chance to address meetings of parents of handicapped children. Sometimes the president of the association gets up and speaks of the "tragedy" of the maladjusted children, and of the government which does not give enough aid, and so on. And, there in the room, I see about ten of these "maladjusted" young people. They know full well that they are the source of this "tragedy" and this anguish of their parents. Sometimes we are tempted to believe that they do not understand. But they do understand well enough to know they are a source of anxiety.

In such a situation, what would *we* do? We would no doubt leave the room after being so insulted. But if we were incapable of moving by ourselves or of crying out, what would we do? We might try and escape into a world of dreams where we could distract ourselves. I have had experience at l'Arche with well-meaning visitors who said in front of our men: "Yesterday I was in a school for normal children." I would like to have said to them: "Do you realise what you are saying? What are Raphael and Philippe going to think? These are men of 39 and 25. Will they not think that they have been rejected from our universe?"

We all know how much we dislike being the cause of discomfort to others. When we are sick, we do not like to show it. We do not want to accept people's care. How much more difficult for the mentally deficient when it is a question of his whole lifetime. Sometimes I pass through the corridors of a hospital and I see the look on a face which says to me: "When I die I will leave a free bed!" In the attitude of the nurse there is often a gesture, perhaps unconscious, which means "You are not important . . . there are many others on the waiting list." The feeling in a man that there is no special place for him in the universe is frightening. I feel this everyday in those with whom I live. You cannot live unless you feel you are in your right place. That place is not necessarily one of efficacity and productivity. It can be in the heart of someone. We begin to feel that inner happiness when we feel certain we are important to someone; that when we die, someone will cry over us; that we will have left an emptiness, not only in a bed but in a heart.

Misery is the repercussion of all the careless, sometimes scornful looks of people who pass through our lives, indifferent to our suffering. There is for example the great suffering of black

America. I take this example because I know it from my experience in the black section of Chicago a few years ago. There was much sadness there. It was not so much the material poverty; many families had some money, and a car. It was much more the feeling that if they wanted to go to such and such an area the whites would move out. Or if a boy wanted to go out with a white girl, then people would talk. And so he says to himself: "I am not like the others. I am not really a man worthy of the name." And when this attitude lasts for generations, when it is the whole atmosphere of a man's environment from childhood up, then he becomes convinced of it. And as long as he is certain he is not a man, he will not really try to live like a man. He will accept filthy living conditions. He will have little interest in anything, nor any desire to do something with his life. He has no motivation other than hate and frustration.

This is the drama of so many of our men, who, having been hurt and made fun of in their childhood, ask us the question: "Do you think I am crazy?" The miserable man feels abandoned. He feels he is of no use, no good. We may say sometimes: "He acts like an animal." But it is not true. Man never acts like an animal. He acts like a sub-animal. The animal always acts according to his state of being. If a man loses all confidence in the dignity of his being, he gives up completely and no longer acts according to his nature. That is why it is useless for well-intentioned people to say to the alcoholic, "You shouldn't drink." That only pushes him deeper into his misery. He knows he shouldn't drink. You don't have to tell him. And when you do he only repeats once more to himself, "I am no good."

The miserable person is also each one of us at different moments of our lives, when we are having difficulty becoming part of a group, or when we are having difficulty living in harmony with others. We may ask, "Who am I? Am I really important? Do I really have any value?" We lose confidence in ourselves, and losing this confidence, we harden our hearts. We no longer dare look reality in the face. We have difficulty sharing. We have difficulty living in communion with others. We flee into another world where we become sad, aggressive, and critical.

Each Man Can Become A Source of Life

What does the miserable person need in order to escape from his misery? The first thing is not necessarily money. If we give money to the alcoholic we know what he will do with it. Perhaps you have read the book of Carolina Maria de Jesus, *Child Of Darkness*. The Book is simply a diary she wrote which someone found and published. Carolina lived in the slums of San Paolo. Day after day she relates her experiences of filth, prostitution and death. It is staggering to read of her experiences. She earned a lot of money from this book, but she spent it all recklessly and returned to her life in the slums. Fundamentally it was not money she needed. The miserable person needs most of all another person who will in some way fill the thirst for union through his presence. The miserable man thinks he is lost and needs someone who understands him so he may regain confidence in himself. He needs someone who says: "I have confidence in you!" . . . someone who will help him to regain life and rediscover lost hope. But that can take a long time. A man who has been hurt, frustrated, and rejected for years will not find new life and confidence immediately. We must go slowly, gently. He needs someone who will give him a little strength, a little energy, a little motivation in small doses which do not extinguish what Isaiah calls: "the vacillating flame" of his life. We must approach him with tenderness and gentleness to reanimate it.

There is a poem by E. E. Cummings in which he says:

"Slowly, slowly, your slightest look will unclose me" but the slightest look will not always unfold the miserable person. Sometimes long years are necessary. I am thinking of some of the men in our homes. It is not *one* look, one act, but years of looks and gestures that they need. They have been bady hurt, just as a young person who has loved once and whose love was rejected or betrayed, he closes himself up. He will not open up to the very next person who says "I love you." He will say "I have suffered too much and I am not going to begin again. I will not open myself up for I have been too wounded. I will wait and see!" He needs a long time before he will have confidence in another.

The miserable man needs a look that comes from our whole being; . . . for words can lie. We can say to someone: "I love you" in a way that means "I am sick of you." There can be discrepancies between words and thoughts, between thoughts and life. The miserable person needs a look of acceptance, not of pity. Pity is something which will only sink the other deeper into his suffering and sadness.

The miserable person needs us to come towards him, not out of duty or through pity, but because he is a human person. He is important, of real value, irreplacable in the eyes of God. It is important that he live . . . if not, something precious will be missing from the universe, a flower will be missing in the garden of

32

humanity . . . he must live . . . But it may take a long time to gain his trust and call him forth. We must then be persevering.

But how to be present to another! Our hearts are so hard. We are so insensitive to the suffering of others. We must pray the Holy Spirit to change our hearts of stone into hearts of flesh so that we may give life, for love is giving of life and liberty. By our confidence in another we can bring forth new aspirations and a taste for life in him. We can help the miserable person to live, to progress and to grow. And he will only begin to want to live when he has been told by our gestures, words, the tone of our voice, our look, our whole being that it is important that he live.

We must be without anguish ourselves if we are to look at him with this spontaneous look of love. We must let drop our defences and be at peace. Only then will we be able to bring forth new life, by our very presence, helping the other to love and to find motivation.

Deep in our hearts there is a call to live in communion with others, a call to love, to create, to risk. But there is also that radical feeling of our poverty when faced with human misery. I am afraid to give myself. I have constructed a world of security around me, . . . so many so-called interests which keep me from communing with others . . . I want to, but cannot. So many things seem to prevent me from loving and I feel them in my inmost being . . . so many defences and fears. I risk losing hope. I risk entering into a world of sadness and I begin to doubt myself. I have doubts about others. I doubt the value of my presence. I doubt everything.

This is our human condition. We want so much but we feel incapable. We believe in love but where is it? There are so many obstacles to break through within ourselves in order to become free and to become present to others; to their misery and to their person.

Our hope is to become freer each day in order to accept others, to be fully present to them. That is our hope. It is only in that way we will be able to give life. Come, Holy Spirit, give us hearts of peace and warmth which can serve as a refuge for those who suffer. Come, help us be present one to another.

Too Long

Too long
have we forgotten
that Peter and John and Eileen
   — mentally deficient —
are people.

People who love
and who want to be loved
who have joys
like you and me.
(You see we are normal people
. . . isn't it nice being normal?)

Peter & John & Eileen
have hearts that suffer
when we do not look at them
with respect
and love.

Too long have they been treated
like perpetual, dependent, incapable
children for whom we must do everything . . .

"poor creatures."
When will we learn,
When will we learn

that Peter & John & Eileen
have their rights
for they are people
and more —
children of God.
We have too long despised them.
We have treated them with pitying paternalism,
ignoring their potentialities.

We have forgotten
that they want
our **respect**
our **love***, but not smothering, protective love,*
but love made up of esteem
and a desire to give life,
possibilities to create,
to give,
to feel useful to society

They have a right
to grow, to develop
in creativity and work
in joyful leisure,
in knowledge,
in small houses,
in spiritual life.

All these activities
should be open to them,
but we the so-called
normal people

(isn't it nice being normal . . . you & me?)

with atrophied hearts
and over-burdened minds,
obsessed by efficacity,
we forget that they are people.

Peter,
John,
Eileen,
You have no voices to cry out.
You cannot go on strike.
Will you forgive society?
Will you forgive me?

For too long
I ignored you.

Christ on the cross
cried out,
"My God, my God, forgive them
for they know not what they are doing."

When you are resurrected
will you say that
to our Eternal Father
for us?
"They did not know what they were doing
when they didn't stop to listen to us,
to respect us,
to help work and live."

(Isn't it nice being normal . . . you and me!)[1]

---

[1]"Too Long", Jean Vanier, Probings Canadian Mental Health Association.

The Place of the Mentally Handicapped in the Modern World

What is the meaning of mental retardation? Do the mentally handicapped have a real place in society? More precisely, have they a role to play in human history and in the future of the world?

I write as a philosopher, but one who has for many years experienced the joy of living continually with the mentally handicapped. My collaborators and I have undertaken to look after about sixty mentally handicapped adults for the rest of their lives. A community has thus grown up, consisting of small "family" groups living in a village.

First I would like to express my gratitude to these men we have gathered together from hostels, psychiatric hospitals, and the streets of Paris. So often they have been looked upon as outcasts, mad, they are despised because they are weak and unable to fend for themselves. They have taught me much about human nature and the real meaning of human existence, the true value of love, of wonder, and even of contemplation.

Those of us who work more or less continually with the so-called "handicapped" are forced to ask ourselves the question: What is a handicapped person? Is such a person a complete human being or not? What is his place in society? Too often these questions are not asked explicity enough but today I want to consider them seriously for our attitude to the "handicapped" must depend on how we answer them.

The problem is an old one: Plato, and even Aristotle with all his humanism, affirm that the weak should be killed at an early

---

'The Place of the Mentally Handicapped in the Modern World' — a talk given to the International Association for the Scientific Study of the Mentally Retarded at Montpellier on 16th September, 1967. Reprinted from Jesus Caritas "The Heart of My Brethren", Winter 1968.

age. For them, if a man was not able to fulfil himself through the use of reason or to work effectively, there was no reason for him to live. Time, energy and money should not be wasted on the care of outcasts. As in the world of art, for each masterpiece there are some failures and these should be eliminated.

The other side of this restricted view of man, where absolute primacy is given to reason, is another concept, that of more spiritually orientated cultures. A friend of mine, the father of a very handicapped child, told me the other day that an Algerian, a Kabyle, on seeing his son at the railway station said: "How lucky you are to have a child like that!" And seeing the father's astonishment he said: "Yes, we believe that a family that has a child like that is blessed by Allah!" Anyone who is handicapped either physically or mentally, is considered in some civilizations to be "religious" (I believe this was the case in ancient China) and to be more in touch with the spiritual. In Greek mythology, madmen were often thought of as prophets. They spoke a strange language, they were in a way intermediaries between man and the gods. In our day these exceptional characteristics of madness and of maladjustment (for in common parlance the two are often confused, though distinct in psychiatry) have been shown in the films of Fellini. Steinbeck, in his book *Of Mice and Men* shows us Lennie, who lives, in a way, outside restrictive social convention. An extraordinary creature, he becomes terrifying in moments of panic. In drug addiction, L.S.D., and in some forms of art is there not sometimes a feeling for the primacy of madness, of the superiority of madness over cold reason?

Between these two extremes, there is what we may call the western humanist attitude. The mentally handicapped are neither to be despised, nor are they to be thought of as being nearer to God or the gods. They are indeed human beings, but incomplete, deficient, weak, infirm, handicapped. We, the normal, the "non-deficient", have no right to get rid of them. (Even if we do not reject them physically, we unfortunately do not hesitate to do so spiritually and psychologically, treating them rather as objects than as persons). They are "poor things" who must be helped and protected; children who will remain so all their lives. They must be given suitable living conditions. And, most important, we must find occupations for them because they can be useful! I have heard someone who specialises in the care of the retarded say that such an individual can only be described as "half a person", a truncated individual who can only half respond whether in terms of work, friendship, or religion. This point of view has produced very good results in the field of work. One has seen quite severely

40

handicapped individuals operating machines, producing quite a good output and earning a reasonable wage. But surely this is not enough!

Then how should we look upon them? Failures to be eliminated? Blessed by God? Paternally with condescension as inferior beings who must be helped? I would like to suggest an attitude which has the advantage of assimilating what is true and obvious in those already mentioned, and which takes account of the attractive qualities which make some retarded people so appealing.

The mentally retarded are certainly failures in the light of reason and responsibility. They are not autonomous, they cannot achieve that freedom which has come to be synonymous with independence. One can go further, as an eminent psychiatrist writes: "The mentally retarded individual is suggestible, naive and easily influenced. His 'self' lacks strength and form. He is weak."

He has undoubtedly a weakness of the "self", that is of the rational and wilful self. This rational self is necessary in order that we may be active in society, capable of organizing our lives and those of others. But man is not just a social being who has to struggle to further his place in society and defend himself, he also loves and wants to be loved, to communicate and to share. To be active in society it is imperative to have a strong and integrated self. But the qualities needed to communicate are not the same. To be admired and to be loved are quite different things. We spontaneously love a child, who is happy, pure, simple, laughing; is it not his youth, his weakness, his innocence and purity which makes us love him?

There are men who are efficacious, who have all the qualities needed to organize, to act and to command, but their hearts are atrophied, they have no compassion. They are too self-reliant and independent. They have cut off part of their personality, the capacity to enter deeply into a relationship with other human beings. They tend to regard other people as objects, or at best as inferior and without value. They are more at ease with documents, materials, with "interesting cases" or with men who must be ordered about like robots, than with someone who is suffering or distressed and who is in need of compassion. They are domineering and their consciousness of self is one of superiority.

Others, in spite of their technical and mental capacity have not allowed their emotions to become cold and rigid, they have been able to preserve that sensibility which allows a man to communicate with, and have compassion for someone else. They are not afraid of human relationships. They have preserved that transparency and purity which make them attractive to others. Their open nature is appealing; a feeling of warmth and goodness emanates from them. Their movements, their expression, their smiles, their way of shaking hands, their behaviour, their tone of voice, far from expressing hardness and aggressiveness, breathe forth gentleness, goodness and understanding. These important qualities which enable a man to accept another person and communicate with him, are found not in the rational self, but in a deeper self which corresponds to an aspiration to love which, however, can be suppressed and buried in the realm of the unconscious.

Man, through his reason and his will, takes his place in society and acts according to the norms of that society. But it is his aspirations towards love which open him to other human beings, inasmuch as they are unique and have within them eternal and infinite potentialities whose depth transcends society, with its conventions and even its laws. It is this love which instead of driving us to dominate others, helps us to feel for a man and identify ourselves with him, to communicate with him with a warmth of self-giving, self-effacement, sacrifice and humility.

You see what I am driving at. The mentally handicapped do not have a consciousness of power. Because of this perhaps their capacity for love is more immediate, lively and developed than that of other men. They cannot be men of ambition and action in society and so develop a capacity for friendship rather than for efficiency. They are indeed weak and easily influenced, because they confidently give themselves to others; they are simple certainly, but often with a very attractive simplicity. Their first reaction is often one of welcome and not of rejection or criticism. Full of trust, they commit themselves deeply. Who amongst us has not been moved when met by the warm welcome of our boys and girls, by their smiles, their confidence and their outstretched arms. Free from the bonds of conventional society, and of ambition, they are free, not with the ambitious freedom of reason, but with an interior freedom, that of friendship. Who has not been struck by the rightness of their judgements upon the goodness or evil of men, by their profound intuition on certain human truths, by the truth and simplicity of their nature which seeks not so much to appear to be, as to be. Living in a society where simplicity has been submerged by criticism and sometimes by hypocrisy, is it not comforting to find people who can be aware, who can marvel? Their open natures are made for communion and love.

They become troubled, and may fall into great distress, in a situation of insecurity. This distress is much greater because they have no rational nature which would help them to overcome and adapt themselves more or less successfully in accordance with conventions and laws. And since no man can live in anguish, they become angry and violent, or sink into a state in which they refuse all contact with reality. Those who care for the mentally deficient in situations where their instinct for love cannot develop note their lack of vitality or aggressive tendencies, as well as their desire for immediate satisfaction in eating and sexuality. On the other hand those who are able to live with them in happy, human conditions, where each one is respected, surrounded by love and treated as a unique person having his rightful place and role to play in the community (and even in the world) observe this weakness but in a different way. They see above all how this weakness leads to a flowering of love. They marvel at their ability to give themselves in purity and innocence, simply and with great joy. They appreciate their capacity for work but above all the friendly atmosphere of their workshops.

In a world which is continually becoming harder, where men are obliged to work furiously to acquire riches, where kindness is not respected and is drowned in a mounting tide of efficiency, the mentally handicapped have an important part to play, because they have time to look and think and marvel and love, they are a continual reminder of the value of community. They are a sign, by their very being, that peace and joy, happiness in fact, are not gained by work alone, and do not depend on wealth. Therefore, they utter a terrible warning; a warning that if men do not use their knowledge and ability to make the world more just, more brotherly, and to bridge the ever-widening gap between rich and poor then this world will end in agony, strife and fire. The mentally handicapped seen in this light, with their very attractive qualities are a constant reminder of the poverty and receptivity required by love, but also of the wonderment, joy and peace which radiate from those who know how to receive and how to give.

Furthermore, the handicapped by his very being is a challenge. His weakness, his openness, his simplicity, his confidence, providing he is placed in conditions that are happy and human, call forth goodness from those who hold power and wealth. For those who are not yet quite hardened, who are still able to be receptive, contact with the handicapped is often a revelation. They have a strange ability to attract; one cannot be unmoved by their lovable simplicity unless one is extraordinarily hardened. The handicapped can in this way form a breach in the walls which we men of the twentieth century have built around ourselves through fear of others. By his very being he can inspire feelings not of pity, paternalism and condescension, but of true altruism.

This is how the mentally handicapped can play his part in society and in the evolution of the world. He restores the balance of the virtues of sensibility and love. He forces society, if it heeds his appeal, to soften the hardness of its technology and administration. If we remain unmoved by the appeal of these weak beings, who need us, then the struggle will continue for it is grounded in the superiority of the rational self, collective or individual. It will then be a race for power, for armaments, for ever more complex techniques. If, on the other hand, society, governments, leaders and each individual instead of trying to rival each other for power and glory, listen to the appeal of the weak and submit to their appeal, while trying to help them, our world instead of becoming more and more dislocated and torn asunder, will be on the way to unity and peace.

No, the mentally handicapped person is not an outcast, a failure; he is a whole person of great importance, for no person is without importance. Through his weakness he constitutes a challenge. Are we, men of the twentieth century, so self-satisfied as not to be revolted by present injustice? Are we too rich, too superior to hear the silent cry of the mentally handicapped?

Strength Lies in Weakness

In these pages, I would like to bear witness to the spiritual and supernatural life of men who, alas, are referred to by society as handicapped, subnormal. I say "alas" because so often these words denote an attitude of segregation. Of course one is obliged — particularly in the medical and psychological fields — to classify disease and psychopathology. But it is vitally important that the words used be free from an undertone of contempt. One can so quickly forget the human person and the respect he needs and see only his psychology, his disease and his social usefulness — or uselessness. Yet the Christian knows — or should know — that the value of a human being rests not in his strength but in the love which inspires his activities. The affectionate and delicate gesture of a so-called "subnormal" man has more value before God and for the world than great human acts carried out with a desire for power and domination. God's ways are not man's ways.

It is true that looking at the mentally handicapped from the point of view of efficiency and usefulness to society, there is little they can contribute. Oh, they can work and even do some very beautiful craftwork — the mosaics and the cushions we make in our workshops are proof of that! But his uniqueness, his most profound value, does not lie there.

Living day after day with our men — we are responsible for 70 adult men and will look after them for life if they wish — I have discovered in them a world of simplicity, purity and goodness. Of course these qualities, often hidden deep in their hearts, can only develop to the extent that they feel secure and live in an atmosphere of work, peace and joy, and where they are respected for their deepest qualities. I have also seen the deep sadness of mentally deficient men and women, when they are closed up in asylums or psychiatric hospitals, just as I have known their possibility for violence if they are not treated as human beings.

45

But when those whom society calls "feeble-minded", or even worse, "idiots", feel they are appreciated, a very harmonious life flows forth, with much confidence and love.

They have taught me more about the gospel and even about human relations than all the great psychological and philosophical concepts; or rather they have allowed me to catch a glimpse of what should be true theology, true philosophy and true psychology. For this I am truly grateful to them. More than this, I have discovered Jesus in them, Jesus radiating goodness, Jesus the mirror of purity, Jesus meek and humble, and sometimes Jesus suffering and in agony. Surely it is because of this, thanks to the gifts of the Holy Spirit, that a firm bond has been formed between them and us, their assistants. These links will last, I am sure, for eternity — links that warm our minds and hearts. And they have brought me much joy and peace. Sometimes people say to the assistants, "It must be depressing to live with the mentally handicapped all day long." Not at all! For myself at least, and for most of us, I think, I can say that I have never been so happy. Of course on occasions we feel discouraged, tired and "fed up", and obviously there are some hard times. Our men have their difficulties, but they are merely like clouds which disappear under the warm sun of friendship and joy.

I think it has been one of the greatest graces of my life (and may Jesus keep me faithful to it!) to meet Him in the hearts of the weak. In the course of my life, I have met powerful men; and if they used their power to serve justice they could be, as it were, images of the power of God. But in the radiation of the weak one touches on another mystery: a divine presence through simplicity and love . . . a tender love, confident and faithful. Who could fail to be touched by the purity of Raphael's expression and his tender gestures as he brings a flower to Mira? By the simple and naive remarks of Philippe about his spiritual experiences? By Michel's humility after a burst of anger? By the confidences imparted by this one or that?

So-called "normal" men often hide their real selves behind a wall of timidity, hardness, and a certain hypocrisy and quest for social esteem. They are almost afraid to show themselves as they are. The mentally handicapped are not like this. Those fortunate enough to know them when they live in a happy atmosphere where they can develop to their full potential, have experienced the gentleness and confidence expressed by their outstretched hands. The defective has nothing to lose. He can show himself as he is, providing of course that no attempt is made to make him live another life than his own. Thus Pierrot, for example, does not hesitate to say to the managing director of a factory who has come to discuss the supply of materials to our workshops and is having lunch with us, "Everybody does the dishes here!" or to a government official who arrives late for a visit, "Why are you late?" Real personal relationships grow up between them and us in which, without fear, each can be himself. Raphael and others of our handicapped friends have helped me to be myself, without fear and without trying to "put on" another personality.

But if, from the point of view of human relations, they have taught me the immense value of qualities of the heart as distinct from those of the mind, it is perhaps mainly at the level of the life of grace and faith that they have opened my eyes and my mind.

As a result of my educational background and my social upbringing, I tended to link the life of faith and supernatural love to my capacities of reasoning and understanding: in order to know the Father, and to live a life of grace, one must do theology and live according to a force of character and will power. This may be true for those who possess certain rational capacities but in living with the handicapped I have discovered that so often Jesus is not tied by our intellectual activity and human capacity.

I have seen the most extraordinary progress in grace and love in men who are very poor humanly and psychologically, who can hardly talk, and who always live on the verge of some crisis or other. I have seen Raphael, radiant with joy. One feels his presence in a group and yet he is severely handicapped. In the past four years he has never, to my knowledge, missed daily Mass and Communion. But he is not under any obligation to go! In fact he is one of the only ones to go to Mass daily. Mass at 7:25 a.m. is too early for many of the others. And Gerard, the difficult 19 year old lad who has spent long years in a psychiatric hospital . . . he has really met Jesus. I remember his baptism and his remark, "Jesus, He really calms you down." And Jean-Claude, a mongol, who has such a simple and real faith. Jean-Michel who gives his money to missionaries. There are so many examples, so many actions, so many gestures which have shown me that when they say the name of Jesus they know of Whom they speak. And they love this Jesus and they are often very docile to His Spirit. Is it because they are not capable of forming ideas of the nature of Christ, of His role in history, that they are freer, more open to simply receive His Presence? I would not necessarily say that, but it seems quite evident to me that, being incapable of formulating theological arguments and often of performing purely voluntary and rational acts, they are very capable of living a life of faith, hope and love. And the simplicity of their faith, the purity of their love, are even greater perhaps because they are not encumbered by ideas and social needs.

47

The mentally retarded has something so true and simple about him. He is not artificial. He may be "coarse" or "common" but perhaps it is this "primitive" and "uncultivated" aspect which is responsible for the fact that his faith is simple and real. Perhaps it is because they live more by the heart than by reason that they are able to receive the presence of Jesus within them. We "normal" Christians, (if there is such a thing) we are so taken up by the reactions and opinions of others arounds us; we are afraid to manifest our faith, afraid to show that we are different . . . not "with it". Our schools must be like others; our industries must be like others. We often have a certain inferiority complex. We are afraid to show ourselves as we are, or should be, disciples of Jesus, the Prophet of the Sermon on the Mount. And do we really believe in Jesus and in His Holy Spirit? How often we lack audacity, joy, confidence. I have found with a good number of the handicapped, that they are not afraid to show who they are nor are they bogged down by social conventions. They have helped me a great deal this way.

I think that many of us, having a certain interior strength, rational capacities and friends, tend to rely on our own capacity. We are not poor as we present ourselves to Jesus. Of course Jesus wants us to develop our qualities and our powers, particularly if we use them for good. But we always run the risk of not surrendering ourselves sufficiently to the Holy Spirit. We rely on our own capacity rather than on God. We are rich. The handicapped frequently have nothing. They are poor. They are not made for power and glory. They seem to be made more for communion and friendship. And because of this the Kingdom of Heaven is theirs. They have often wept and thus they will be comforted; they have been persecuted and despised and so they will find love. Give them proper living conditions which are humane, harmonious, and they will flower, and God willing, grace will blossom within them.

The grace of Jesus is given in a very special way to the weak. Our boys have really taught me the value of these words of St. Paul: "Consider, brethren, the circumstances of your own calling; not many of you are wise, in the world's fashion, not many powerful, not many well born. No, God has chosen what the world holds foolish, so as to shame the wise. God has chosen what the world holds weak, so as to shame the strong. God has chosen what the world holds base and contemptible, nay has chosen what is nothing, so as to bring to nothing what is not in being; no human creature should have any ground for boasting in the presence of God." (Cor. 1, 26-29)

The greatest suffering of the mentally handicapped is to feel "different" and "useless." He needs friends who will help him to discover his own personality and his place in society, friends who love him and respect him. But most of all he needs the Love of God which he may discover through them. If, through faith and especially by experiencing the presence of Divine Love in himself he can discover how much Jesus really loves him, then I venture to say he is no longer handicapped. He may have difficulty in finding his place in society, but knowing the love of Jesus for him, he discovers his own personality and his real significance in the world. As he cannot marry like others, he will find fulfilment for his affection in moments of rest near Jesus, the best of all friends. If a spiritual life is a necessity for every man, it is especially necessary for the weak and for those who cannot find human fulfilment. Even more than others they have the right to receive the truths of faith and especially a knowledge of Jesus Christ by and in love, fraternity, prayer and silence. Their religious life will not primarily be one of action but rather that of contemplation — that is, the life of one who welcomes Love on earth, who receives peace and radiates it and who lives a life nourished by prayer.

Obviously one must not exaggerate; the mentally defective is not a saint simply because he is handicapped. But this weakness and deficiency, far from excluding him from the grace of God, constitute as it were a direct appeal to divine mercy. It is up to us "normal" Christians to recognize this and put ourselves at their service, at the service of the Holy Spirit in them. They need us so as to receive Love . . . and we need them. For this of course we must believe in the Spirit and also in them. The psychological defects of our boys may try us sorely. We tend often to forget that Jesus is in them and that they are sons of God, called to live eternally face to face with our Father. Our community is not a religious community and our assistants are not necessarily fervent Christians —it is sufficient that they love and profoundly respect our boys. There is simply a common spirit which animates us and a Christian inspiration at the source of the community. But this spirit implies above all respect for the liberty of each one. It is a question of creating a climate and a situation where each one may discover himself and be himself, where he may, when the time comes, and in all freedom, meet Christ; where he may also meet his brother and play his part as a human person in a true and positive way in the world and the movement of history.

At l'Arche we are trying to establish small houses of eight handicapped men or boys and one or two assistants. It is a question of creating an atmosphere where mentally handicapped men (and soon, I hope, women) can live their lives as happily as possible; working, making the most of their time of leisure, developing according to the deepest aspirations of their being. It is a question of creating a truly human community where they can find the necessary security in order to progress in every human and spiritual domain; particularly where their hearts can be allowed freely to develop in love for their brothers and for God; a place where they can taste the eternal joys, often silent and peaceful, of a fraternal life in the presence of Jesus.

Jesus, make my heart ever gentler and more humble, so that I may remain ever present to those You have confided to my care, and in this way make me an instrument of Your Love which gives life, joy and real freedom.

Innocence

The innocent one

    is he who has done no harm to anyone . . .
    he may have been accused of it,
        unjustly, wrongly,
        but he has proven his innocence.

The innocent one

    is he in whom no evil resides;
    his heart is not divided . . .
        in him there is no duplicity,
        no deviation in his words,
        in his actions . . .
        he has but one look,
        that of love
        and of gift of self . . .
        he gives of himself unboundingly.

The innocent one

    has committed no evil,
    is very different from the virtuous person
        who believes he is good
        because he has followed
        the letter of the law
        and thinks he is pure
        because of it . . .
        pure according to the law
        but perhaps impure according
        to the Spirit.

The innocent one
is the child . . . his candour, his simplicity,
one who likes to play,
who easily throws himself into the arms of others;
this little one in whom no evil resides,
does not see the evil in others
but has confidence in them.
And the child,
innocent, candid, open,
is a pole of attraction: no one fears him
for there is no malice in him:
"I am not afraid of you,
I can come to you without fear,
you have no prejudices.
Your eyes, clear and limpid,
break into ashes the barriers that I have
built around my heart,
barriers of fear . . .
your innocence calls me forth."
But this child,
Is he truly innocent?
Is not his innocence sometimes cajoling?
"Alas, your innocence is so often impure
for you are seeking my affection . . .
trying to seduce . . .
your limpidity is no longer a source of life
for you wish to draw me to you
in order to reassure you and give you security . . .
this is part of your call."

The innocence
of he whose reason is not developed,
who is not important in the city of men,
nor powerful, nor really efficient;
nor capable of choosing, of harming, of destroying,
is still different . . .
his innocence will radiate especially
when he feels our confidence, our respect and
our love.
His lack of autonomy makes him seek harmony and
unity
with us; desiring to melt in this union
without losing himself . . . the strange clearness
in his confiding eyes,
the naivety in his laughter.

This innocence,
    like that of a child,
    can lead to a dream world, a utopia,
        for there is the risk that we want too much
        to protect this innocence
        and do not really believe in the value of his person,
        in his capacity to choose and to grow;
        we close him up into the world of dreams
        and ourselves with him.
        He becomes a curious object in a world of hate;
        people may come from afar to see this phenomenon:
        a museum piece in a corrupted world . . .
        perhaps we want to guard that innocence too much
        and so fail to see the person who is,
        and must grow.
        But this candid, limpid innocence has a real
        eternal value;
        it is a transcendant sign,
        a touch of the infinite,
        an appeal for clarity,
        a precious flower in humanity,
        not a museum piece.

There is also the innocence
    of one who has been protected,
    who refuses contact with the world and men . . .
        and who builds a pure and clean world
        but a world which is illusion . . .
        he closes himself into this protected world,
        not wanting to be soiled by the mud of reality
        which surrounds him.
        His innocence is made of fear,
        fear of dirtying himself . . .
        it is not love.
        Innocence is not true innocence
        until it is completely directed towards love.

There is also the innocence
    of he who daily walks side by side with evil,
    who lives near it,
        who through his actions, his look,
        through the silence of his peace,
        transforms evil . . .

He takes this evil into his own flesh
and transforms it through the guiding hand
of the Spirit,
saving, communicating that peace
which overflows within him
and which he cannot contain:
the dikes collapse under the weight of love.
His acts and gestures may be condemned:
as Jesus who transgressed the Sabbath
and the prophet who revolts against
hypocrital habits for the sake of
the eternal law of love . . .
and in so doing he identifies himself
with those in misery
and he communicates the fire that consumes him . . .
but the world cannot accept this innocent man,
his presence is condemning . . .
the clarity of his eyes,
not like those of a child
who seek to captivate and seduce,
not like those of him who is ignorant and naive . . .
but those of a man who knows the extent of his actions,
who knows that before men and the law
he may be considered crazy
or maybe condemned . . .
but he chooses to let himself be drawn by this
eternal law of the person
of love
of truth . . .
he is a free man . . .
free from conventions,
     free from his own flesh, in the sense of St. Paul,
     for he has been transformed by the gentle touch
     of the Spirit from on high,
     surging up within him.
Society does not like people who are completely free
for it feels judged by them . . .
     they can not be classified into certain social groups
     as society likes so much to do.

The innocent one is a free person
     who has become slave to the Spirit.
     He is not chained to any group,
          white or black,
          with their social conventions,
          with their "acceptable" ways of doing things.

The Spirit gives him a universal heart
which enables him to meet the miserable person,
      the rich,
      the poor,
      the handicapped
      with a loving heart,
      welcoming them into his own heart
      and introducing them to this breath
      of Eternal within . . .
This innocence one
is able to grasp in a mysterious way
      the innocence that is hidden in the heart
      of those whom social conventions call "sinners";
      there is the innocence of the prostitute,
      the delinquent,
      the thief,
      which remains hidden
      in the darkness of anguish and worry
      and which responds to the calling forth
      of a look from the innocent.
      Mary-Magdalene,
      the good thief.

In the depth of their beings,
there is an untouched secret,
      they do not think they are better,
      they are waiting for that love
      that will save them . . .
      and call them forth,
      they are awaiting the innocent one.

He who believes he is master,
      or the first,
      or a doctor of learning,
         or pure
         or in need of no one
         risks losing his secret innocence,
         turning away from the regard of the innocent,
         condemning him even,
         but in so doing condemns himself . . .

True innocence
      is like a cloak which comes from God.
      But then again it is not like a cloak
         for it does not envelop externally,

but rather rises forth from deep within
and spreads out as waves
which break forth over cupidity and pride,
and the infernal need to possess
present in us
and which encrusts and covers
our initial innocence.
This initial, true innocence
is the innocence of love
which gives of itself without fear,
knowing one is loved and enveloped
in the love of the Father:
and that first source is Jesus.

The innocent person
    espouses the misery of others,
      becoming one with them
           without losing himself.

The innocent person
    is he who is guilty only of having revealed
    to the so-called "virtuous"
        the impurity of their hearts.

The innocent person
    cannot hurt or destroy . . .
    on the contrary,
        his look touches the depths,
        wounding, transforming and calling forth
        the sources of goodness hidden there . . .
        it is only he who closes his heart and rejects
        the call of the innocent,
        who enters into the realms of stagnation and death.

And you, the innocent
    you are not afraid,
        you are not afraid of the world;
        nor of evil,
        nor of others,
        nor of yourself and your own flesh . . .
        you walk through life without fear, looking . . .
        giving of yourself with such tranquillity,
        your face limpid and radiant . . .

but you do not radiate your own innocence,
that is why you are not afraid. . . .
>you are not afraid of losing it . . .
>for you know that your innocence comes from above,
>from a deeper source than your own self:
>innocence which bursts forth from God
>and is called Jesus.

It is because you are poor and you know it,
and because you love your poverty,
>that you are able to approach life,
>the world,
>others,
>without fear,
>to give of your innocence,
>to bring peace,
>that certitude and strength of love . . .

You, the innocent one,
>you can touch the world, matter, and others,
>not taking them for yourself,
>>nor tearing them away from another,
>>nor trying to possess them:
>>— (impure and possessive touch) —
>>nor destroying or crushing them
>>to make them disappear or die
>>— (touch of hate and violence) —
>>but to communicate life and liberty
>>which flow from peace . . .

your touch then
becomes like the touch of Jesus,
>a touch of gentleness, and tenderness,
>that burns and cures and gives new life . . .
>"O delicate touch that transforms death into life"
>(St. John of the Cross.)

But people do not want your touch
they reject it, condemning you . . .
>"I send you out," says Jesus,
>"like lambs in the midst of wolves . . .
>be as clever as the serpent,
>as candid as the dove . . ."

But this innocent cannot live for long amongst wolves,
he must necessarily be persecuted and die,
          he is too pure;
          and because he is scorned,
          persecuted,
          poorly considered,
          he will lose the clarity and purity of his eyes.

"He is without beauty, without majesty
Nothing attracts in him ... (Is. 53)
          His limpid eyes become sorrowful eyes;
          His flesh, an anguished and suffering flesh ...
          He loved
          and wanted to give of himself
          in this world of evil,
          in order to transform this evil,
          or rather those engulfed in it;

He came until his own, those he loved but they did not accept him;
He was struck, and brought low
          pierced and wounded,
          led to the slaughter-house like a lamb ...
          like a sheep that is dumb before its shearers,
          never opening his mouth ...

He who had done no wrong
and from whose mouth came no lie
          has been crushed.
          But he offers his life in atonement,
          and from his death will flow waters
          which will communicate the flame of his innocence
          and bring forth new hope ...
          the hope of the innocent
          who keeps his innocence to the end ...
          and who dies on the cross,
          his arms wide open to men,
          but who does not really die
          because the flame of innocence can
          never be extinguished."

But where are you innocent one?
Do you really exist?
          Have I really seen you?
          I am waiting for you
          to transform my whole being
          and call me forth.

Innocence,
a mirage which disappears as soon as I look for it,
for one cannot look for innocence,

It exists,
but only in the degree
that I meet you,
my brother,
my sister,
and you
Jesus,
whom I love.

Integrity in Public Life

Speech delivered at National Prayer Breakfast,[1] Ottawa
— before members of the Canadian Parliament and
Others on June 7, 1967 — during the days of the Israeli-
Arab six day war, three months after the death of
Governor-General George P. Vanier.

I was very moved to be asked to speak to you this morning
because this meeting is very important. May God give me the
grace and the light not to be a disappointment to you who have
invited me.

I am moved also because of the seriousness of the hour. We
are here, men and women in high office, responsible men in Government, to spend a few minutes together thinking about things
that are eternal and we know that not far away from us, war is a
giant force. When men fight we must feel deeply. Our responsibility is always to be where men are suffering. And to be with
those others, the women and children, who always suffer as a
result of war.

I am moved also because this is our Centennial year and we all
realize that this Centennial is not the end of a period, not something that we lean back on. We are going forward. It is a beginning, a beginning for deeper unity.

I would like to begin by saying also that it is moving for me to
be here today because as you know, I had expected to be speaking
before my beloved father. When I went to see him in February,
two days after having received from your President the invitation

---

[1]This talk was given by Dr. Jean Vanier at the Third National Prayer
Breakfast held in the Parliament Buildings, Ottawa, on June 7, 1967, during
the Israeli-Arab six day war and three months after the death of the
Governor-General.

to come to you today, I spoke about it to father and we smiled together about it. Normally, he was the one who would speak in public but today he is silent, having attained a deeper silence and a deeper peace than the one that he had during his wonderful pilgrimage on earth. And maybe I can say today a few things that I couldn't have said if he had been with us. I don't think anybody would have been more surprised than he at the acclamation and the reaction throughout Canada, from Europe and even from Asia, the days following his peaceful and gentle death. Frequently, after a tour through Canada or after speaking in some place where he had been particularly well received, he would come back to the house and say in a sort of surprised manner that the people had accepted him. I think that he would have been the first to have been surprised at those acclamations.

To begin with, I would like to try and show some of the more secret and rather unknown aspects of his life, and which perhaps will give us the key to why he was so loved.

As a man of 79, he remained young — young in heart, young in spirit. He was never old and I would like to try to show where he found the inspiration for his youthfulness, his force and his courage in facing difficult problems.

In reading the books that were beside his bed at the time of his death, and noting the passages that he had lined and under-lined and the notes he had made in the margins, I found a clue to some of these qualities. In one of the books the following passage was underlined heavily: "There is no use arguing about it, you are going to be asked to give daily to the combination of these three exercises: prayer, reflection and spiritual reading. No matter how busy you are, no man is too busy to eat; neither is any man too busy to feed his soul. And if we starve our souls, we will deprive our lives, busy though they may be, of their fruitfulness." I think Dad with extraordinary fidelity maintained that attitude through-out his life. You know that at Rideau Hall he installed a chapel where he attended mass every day. But do you know that every day above that, with strict regularity, he spent half an hour in the chapel, just thinking, and reflecting before his much-loved God. This was where he found his inspiration. He used to remain there even if he had been through difficult periods, even if he was very tired. I remember sometimes going into his room at 10 or 11 o'clock at night after he had had a busy day and he would be sitting in a chair quietly, his hands crossed and with a small sign of his hand he would make me understand that I could come back later because he was having his half hour rendevous with his God.

The other day I found one of the letters that he wrote a few days before he had been installed as Governor-General. It was written to a nun who had given her whole life to prayer and I thought I might give you the contents of this letter, which as you can imagine are deeply private. I feel, now that Dad has gone — though he is still with us in a sense — he would permit me to read you parts of this letter which I found deeply moving. He had a great sense of his own weakness and yet of his strength, not because he felt strong himself but he was strong because he believed in God and in the power of prayer. "Know that your prayers are indispensible, for without the prayers of those who love me I would be seized with pain and I could not bear at my present age to undertake the responsibilities which await me. Knowing as I do, that I lack the necessary strength, I could only hope that my very weakness will save me. I say therefore to Jesus, 'I place my heart in Yours, do with it as You will, may it beat in tune with Your heart, if that should be Your wish; but if not, may it be consumed in the power of Your love.' Pray that He may grant me this grace, without which I will never be able to accomplish the mission which He has confided to my wife and to myself. Ask Him to give me the strength, His strength from day to day, sufficient unto each day. Until now He seems to bestow His grace upon me in this way. Just sufficient strength to meet each day's requirements. I also have the impression, and I hope I am not being presumptuous in thinking so, that He keeps me, as it were, on a leash. There are times when I feel very strong and sure of myself, especially in public, and this is important in front of others. But there are other moments when I am overwhelmed with the feeling of my weakness and impotency. In these moments of weakness, when Jesus pulls upon the leash to remind me of my nothingness, I say to Him, 'I abandon myself to Your merciful love' and yet I know that my abandonment is far from complete, my confidence far from perfect. Pray then, my beloved friend, that Christ will give me the Grace to believe that He will give me that perfect faith which realizes that Jesus will never forsake me. I am, as it were, like Saint Peter trying to walk on the surface of the water. To conclude, I can only say, 'May His will be done.' My term of duty as Governor-General is to be of a five year duration. It will be for Jesus to decide how long I will be able in weakness to serve Him and to serve my country."

Beside his bed lay such books as *Abandonment to Divine Providence* by Father de Caussade, a Jesuit; *The Spiritual Works of John of the Cross,* and the autobiography of the young Carmelite who died at the age of 24, Thérèse of Lisieux, which he had read six times since 1961, the last reading, he had noted at the end of the book, in January of this year. In these books, along with others, especially in the Holy Bible, he found his spiritual nourishment. Theological treatises and discussions, all that appeared complicated in this domain, were distasteful to him. He

64

had a definite inclination to simple truths, that attracted the heart even though they may not stimulate reason. He was so convinced that the prime unique values of life were love, service and the gift of self, that anything that came to endanger these values was immediately rejected.

In Canada my father had the reputation of great moral integrity. This is profoundly true. He had almost a physical horror of anything that smelled of misuse of power and position, anything that tasted of bribery and corruption. He always upheld the right and the just, yet was profoundly loving and merciful to those who humbly recognized their faults and errors and tried to do better. He held in high esteem all those who stood courageously by their principles and gave themselves to noble causes. I am sure it was in prayer that he found the inspiration necessary to always uphold the right and the good, to resist all temptation of pride and misuse of power, and to encourage those who gave themselves to high ideals.

Let us now turn our gaze from my father to the world of political affairs and the reason why we are here. Let us think of the belief that we have in the necessity of prayer. First of all we can say that the example of my father at least shows that faith and prayer will never be a detriment to success in public affairs. On the contrary, prayer will give maturity and judgment, deeper insight, deeper vision, a deeper goodness and kindness and a greater mercy. Today we know well the crisis of our times. We know, all of us, the gravity of the situation, but I sometimes wonder why it is in our country from East to West, that the world of public affairs, the world of politics is so often decried, caricatured and laughed at. Why is it so often you hear people say, "I will not soil my hands with politics but I would rather go into business and science." And yet, what greater vocation is there for men than to assume their responsibilities in national and international affairs? What greater vocation is there than to assume one's responsibilities for the furthering of justice throughout all countries? There is nothing greater, nothing more noble than to be inspired by this feeling of justice and peace, to radiate this justice and peace by the laws of our land and through international organizations. Yet so frequently one hears, "I wouldn't soil my hands." Why? Is it because throughout the land, the example of parliamentary life does not always lead our countrymen, the young, particularly the students, to believe that the parliamentary life is immediately ordained to the good of the country over and above the good of individual parties? Is it because they do not always find in the representatives of the people men motivated by a great ideal of justice, of peace and of wisdom? Maybe it is the very complexity of political life, the strain under which our leaders are put that incites us to fall into ruts of resignation, preventing us from seeing the noble ideals which should govern our endeavours. Isn't this the reason why frequently the young are dismayed? Why do they not find before them the models necessary to go forward in justice, in peace and with a deep desire to help all men, and especially the poorest? Never before has our world been in such need of men of vision, men of courage, men of strength, men who surpass their private, personal ambitions looking only to one thing — to serve our country and to serve mankind. The world is going through one of the deepest and gravest crises of its history. This present crisis is one of transition. We are leaving an era of smug complacency for one of rapid change and technological innovations.

This crisis is affecting all our lives, affecting our society and our families, and it is coupled with deep distress and anxiety. Many, at the sight of so much evil, strife and war, are wondering if man is not only thoroughly stupid but also fundamentally evil. We talk about peace and unity, but how many men today throughout our world are, on the contrary, either at war or actually preparing for war? We know full well the possibilities of destruction that are in our hands. The seriousness of internal problems and the gravity of the hour are very evident. We just have to look at some of the things that are happening throughout our world to realize that the next twenty, thirty or forty years if we are still here, will be the gravest for mankind. Consider the wars that are being waged today, the sore spots throughout the world, the famine, particularly in parts of Asia, the future of the countries of Africa, the dangers of violence in the United States. and in South America, the enigma of China.

Science is on the point of making stupendous discoveries in the domain of genetics, psychiatry, energy, space and electronics. Will man be capable of assuming these discoveries for peaceful purposes in the service of justice? Or will, as so often has been the case, these discoveries be used for purposes of pride, hatred, division and war?

Certainly, amidst these difficulties and disasters, there are reasons for hope: mankind aspiring towards unity, different churches aspiring to unity, noble endeavours, in favour of justice and peace, so many young people devoting themselves to noble tasks in Canada and outside. But alas, as poisonous situations grow, the need for wise and devoted men becomes greater. In this tumultuous struggle, in this vast movement of history, in these interactions of rival civilizations, and in the dynamic application of the revolutionary discoveries of science, Canada has her role to play. She has a magnificent vocation in the family of nations. Many from all parts of the world turn to her in the chaos of our times. Born of two great European cultures, living in close harmony next to the vast United States, fraternally linked to Africa, open towards the East through the Pacific, she has the confidence of all. But how should we play our role?

Here are some of the problems of our times and we ask "What do we need?" We need men of vision, who can feel the pulse of history, who try to prepare for the future. The man in public affairs is not just he who tries to settle conflicts once they have broken out. The statesman must be able to feel the pulse of our time, seizing the profound and new aspirations of modern man, preparing for tomorrow conditions for greater peace and harmony and justice. Thus he must foresee possible causes of strife and eliminate them while they are still in the bud, before they become irreversible and out of human control. He will not live from day to day but he will look into the future, cultivating a deep sense of history and a belief that man can control his destiny and need not be a helpless victim of circumstances. "Si tu n'y prends garde ta vie peut se passer sans toi; si tu n'y prends garde, l'histoire peut se forger sans la pensée humaine." A statesman is neither pessimistic nor optimistic but simply realistic, not blinded by a mirage of success and prestige, not blinded by false values of economy and technology but rather open to the deep and real values of man, those that are lasting and which vary little with the passage of history. These are the values that bring individual, social and international peace, and flowing from peace, bring beauty, goodness, truth and love to individual persons, to communities and to nations, permitting all to attain their fulfilment and profound happiness. Peace and happiness are things that come from inside us. But how do we orient our land, our people; how do we orient countries to a destiny of peace and of justice and fraternity? Where can we find the necessary vision? Where can we find the help and courage and the strength of our own convictions?

Permit me here to quote a passage of a speech given by my father in 1952 at the Catholic University of Paris:

"What sort of spiritual development does our modern world need? Will spiritual values, to repeat a term which has often been used, be sufficient in themselves to re-establish balance and harmony in our universe? I think not and I believe that as Catholics we must have the magnanimity to concede that our world needs not just 'spiritual values' but *genuine* spirituality, the only spirituality deserving of the name, that of the Holy Spirit. Man's intellect left to itself is incapable of creating unity in this immense universe. The giant is too big to be formed and unified by man's intellect alone. God must give us His Spirit and man must transcend himself to participate in the Spirit of the Almighty.

67

To establish unity around us, to carry unity and therefore peace to others we must be in a state of peace and harmony with ourselves. A man divided within himself can sow only the seeds of disunity and war. Only the Spirit of God, Creator of both matter and spirit, source of both truth and love, can bring harmony from such diversity. Our world longs for this vital and profound unity, for we know that without it we will perish.

Our word has an urgent need for a 'spiritual élite.' But we can and must be even more precise than that, for the world needs above all an 'élite of God, an élite of spiritually minded men of God,' who have been formed by God, who have been students in God's school and who, thereafter, are able to radiate His Spirit. These spiritually minded men of God are the friends of God, those with whom God has entered into intimate contact, whom He makes a part of His Spirit. They are the contemplatives and the saints. It is they who must bring to our world this qualitative element, this factor of indispensable unity so that the world may find harmony therein."

I beg that each one of us today may take stock of the seriousness of the situation and the gravity of our own responsibilities. Will it not be in prayer that we can find the vision necessary to disentangle ourselves from the immediate and to look forward to the future; to have the vision and the insight necessary to see how we can orient humanity to real goals of justice, friendship and fraternity? Will it not be in prayer that we will find the strength necessary to remain faithful to our convictions? Not to be bogged down with what others might think, but to be men, steadfast in our own convictions, strong in our hearts, standing close to the principles in which we believe. And so, my friends, may we take stock at this Prayer Breakfast. In a few moments, we will return to our occupations, perhaps uttering hard, humiliating words, frequently trying to break others in order to gain power. Let us take stock of our presence here. The grandeur of the occasion, the sublimity of the prayers, do they not oblige us to reflect upon what all this means and implies? May I suggest that there may be a danger that in a few minutes we will be back on the floor of the House with slaughtering words, back in industry or in our professions with quick and sometimes cruel reactions. Of course, competition, hard discussion, are vital necessities to free government and private enterprise. The party system is an excellent source of valid and thoughtful action, but how often do we speak only to wound the opponent, to slay him, defame him, make him a laughing stock. How eager we are to profit from every opportunity to humiliate. Power attained through humiliating others, and not through the radiation of one's own personal goodness and wisdom and foresight carries the seeds of its own destruction.

This Prayer Breakfast should give each one of us the deep and real conviction that our lives and consciousness should be put under the light of eternal values. Only in the degree that we disentangle ourselves from the temporal and the immediate will we be able to have a clear vision of the evolution of history and of the universe; only then will we be able to perceive the solution to conflicts. Prayer is that peaceful contemplative look towards eternity, and above all, union with the Eternal and receptivity of the spirit of God. Here is the answer. We must be filled with this spirit of eternal love and wisdom. Only in communion with God over and above all time will we find the light, the courage, and the love to accomplish our task and our vocation. Otherwise, this Prayer Breakfast will be but a hypocritical farce, a stunt for the gallery, something to which we came because it was the thing to do. We should come here because we are convinced, and we should leave here even more convinced. If that conviction is not in our hearts and does not put itself into the practice of prayer, of putting one's heart and one's mind and one's spirit into eternal values, values that transcend time, then this Prayer Breakfast will be a hypocritical event. But, it should not be that. It should be a beginning of a new life for each one of us, where we put the desire to do justice and to bring peace into every walk of life. We must bring new life to those who are dying spiritually throughout our land.

Prayer is not the unthinking mumbling of meaningless words, but the opening of our hearts to the Eternal Love that is the source of all creation. Prayer is the response of the heart, to God who is Love. Prayer is the opening of one's heart to peace, to the peace of God, the opening of one's mind and one's heart to the Spirit of God. Prayer is the desire that we might be filled with this spirit of love and of justice and of peace. It is the offering of ourselves to God, who is Love, that we might become the poor instruments of His love; that we might radiate throughout our land and to everyone we know the peace, the compassion, the sweetness, the tenderness and the mercy of God. We all have, we know, a huge thirst for the spirit of God. We all have a thirst for the love of God. Against the problems we face, our weakness is so great. That's why we should go humbly before God and say "Give me your spirit. I am very weak. Help me in my decisions. The seriousness and the gravity of the hour demand it. I only desire one thing, that is, that You will give peace and gentleness. Give the truth of Your Love. Help me. Give strength to my poverty, give strength that I may be courageous in front of others. Give me Your spirit."

Ladies and gentlemen, if we want to be logical in our faith, authentic in our inspirations and sincere in our presence here, then we must leave this breakfast with the firm and steadfast resolution to give at least some few moments each day to prayer, and to ask inspiration and help before every important decision, to spend a few days every year more especially consecrated to letting eternal values penetrate our lives. And may I suggest that this prayer is not an added luxury in our lives, something spiritual to give greater insight, but an absolute necessity. Without prayer we will never be able to accomplish the vast and important task we are called to play in Canada and in the world. This Prayer Breakfast should be a beginning towards that. That every day we may turn towards our God and our Creator and say "Give me Your spirit. I thirst after You because without You, without You in me, I will perish. I will be unable to be an instrument of peace and of justice."

I will be leaving you tonight, and this land that I love, to return to the men I'm responsible for. May I ask you to pray that I may be faithful and constant in my vocation and you may be sure that on my side, I will always keep you in my heart, that you too may be faithful to your vocation. Let all of us then, say deeply and firmly "Je crois". I believe in man; I believe in the dignity of man; I believe that every man can love and is capable of loving; I believe in God and I believe that if we ask God, He will give us His spirit. May we always have the courage to say in our hearts, "I believe." May all of us, if we are of the wonderful race of Abraham, say proudly but yet with deep humility, "I am a Canadian, I am a Jew", and if we are among the disciples of the Prophet of the Mount, "I am a Canadian, I am a Christian."

Education Towards Peace and Universal Brotherhood

Peace in our world is seriously threatened, and not only peace but the very life of the human race. If a world war broke out today, we have such weapons that the whole of mankind is in danger of annihilation. It is therefore urgent that young people be educated for peace and universal brotherhood in a radically new way.

Before going into immediate practical questions of pedagogy — a pedagogy that must be new for we are dealing with a new generation of young people with new demands — let us try to see some of the problems of our time as seen by the young. This will help us to better understand their demands and their needs. We could then attempt to find the type of education needed to encourage the young to work effectively towards the peace to which we all aspire.

1. YOUTH BEFORE THE MODERN WORLD

The young no longer follow, obediently and without question, the traditional values of morality and religion. This is one of the most evident phenomena of our time. There is a crisis in the domain of moral authority.

Previously, societies were dominated or inspired by religious values which exerted influence on the whole concept of the family, on the mores, on the relationship between man and woman, on the whole life style, and on the way in which man accepted, without question and even without sorrow, his lot in life.

These societies are evolving now towards the primacy of economy and technology. Religion and the spiritual life are relegated to the last place; perhaps they have value for the individual, but they have no importance for the organization of men in society.

So often, traditional religious values seem to the young to have nothing to do with life; they are but rituals which are yokes or prisons, and not sources of hope, truth and life. Indeed, blind acceptance of these values seems to keep man in a childish state, and prevents him from seeing evident truths which would help him to evolve more humanly.

These religious values were often perpetuated by the ruling class, rich and powerful, which instead of seeking to make the whole population grow towards a more equal sharing of goods and possibilities of progress, tended to maintain the *status quo,* while giving charitable aid to this or that suffering member or group. The upper classes refused to make the radical change in their way of life by which they would share with the poor and the afflicted, and help them to achieve, themselves, a more human way of life.

The young label as hypocritical all traditions which do not follow the inner logic of fraternity, love of the poor and mystical union with God. They reject all the old values which seem too organized and which do not inspire life. They refuse a moral code which is thrown at them from "on high", and which seems to oppress and suffocate. They want to live; they want to be free. They have seen too many believers saying their prayers, performing their religious duties and moralizing, but living as if they did not really believe in the love of God.

The young respect authenticity and universality. They don't want any contradiction between what one says and what one does. They do not want arbitrary authority, based on rank or function instead of on the intrinsic value of the person. They want truth. They want people to be themselves, without fear. They do not judge according to a system of values or categories; the young are open, accepting and tolerant. What they want is to find men who act out of personal conviction and not out of what people think or say of them.

The young are searching for something which is universal. They don't want just the local, the regional or even the national; they see further than borders.

The young are not materialistic; they are on the contrary in search of an ideal but they want to attain this ideal without a period of formation and maybe without effort; it must be immediate, total, obvious, clear.

The young are disillusioned by technological values and by our consumer society, just as they refuse religions which are not life giving. To produce so as to eat, and to eat so as to produce; to make money so as to spend it: these seem to them to be void of all meaning.

The former moral values which regulated the family and a whole way of life have been replaced most often by the desire to increase one's wealth. Static traditions have been in many cases replaced by fierce activity which induces people to overwork themselves to the point where they no longer see any joy in life.

The consumer society seems to be tied to a new form of tradition which only replaces the old one. We want to appear rich just as before we wanted to appear virtuous. We have kept all the class taboos, the social conventions and the prejudices, but now all is based on the symbols of wealth: cars, golf clubs, swimming pools.

This materialistic society replaces the myths of religion, "opium" of the people, with the myths of publicity, which is but a different form of "opium". False needs are created, along with a new set of values; all forms of trickery are used to sell products; people are encouraged to buy on credit and become shackled in the worst form of slavery, that of debt.

The young are disillusioned by the past; they refuse to accept the divisions created by it; they want a new society of people living in peace, justice and love. They don't want any more wars, even though some of them might start a revolution to attain what they hope would be lasting peace. They refuse the divisions between superior and inferior countries, races, religions, and sexes. They want a united world in which men and women live in a spirit of fraternity, and in which all people can sing, dance and celebrate life.

History has created and prolonged divisions. It has allowed man to dominate woman, father to dominate son, management to dominate labour, upper classes to dominate lower classes, powerful countries to dominate weaker countries, one religion to dominate another, the strong to dominate and exploit the weak.

The young are thirsting for a new society, where there will be neither black nor white, rich nor poor, strong nor weak, but where

74

each person will be accepted because of himself, for his value as a human being.

The young have lost faith in politics. To join a political party is to condone the system which is itself false. The parties are no longer relevant, as a result of their own traditions and organization. They are obliged to accept the values of the present society, and are thus unable to understand the new direction which society must take.

Revolution is therefore necessary, either through non-violent rejection of present injustices, or else violent revolution. A radical change is necessary. Humanity can continue no longer in the economic system of today. The injustices of the rich countries which favour the wealthy, are as inacceptable as the injustices of the socialist countries who favour the strong, those who are in the party, those who will sell their souls and personal freedom for power and comfort.

The young want neither traditional communism, nor the major political parties of the West. Neither one of these truly seeks the good and liberty of all people. Young people are attracted by anarchy and by Maoist-inspired revolutionary movements, for these movements appear less organized and less structured; or else they refuse to participate at all in political affairs.

The young are lost; their ideal is not understood by their elders; and they do not know how to go about forming this new society. Their disenchantment is getting more and more evident, just as evident as the truths to which they aspire. Their cry is a cry for truth and a cry for help. But in front of this truth stands a huge and terribly complex machine: the machine of our society that implies work, factories, unions, business, finance, governments, elections, the majority's need for security, political parties, police, army, international affairs. The ideal of the young appears weak and fragile when confronted by this seemingly immovable monster.

It is easy to criticize the young: "they are idealistic", "it's wonderful but impossible." And we distrust their movements because we fear that international powers are using them to cause trouble and to work their way into the affairs of the country so as to be able later to establish control by some form of tyranny.

And youth, misunderstood by many of those adults who have responsibilities in the world, is itself without leaders. They are like a huge flock without a shepherd, who gather round a few singers who sing of love, universal peace and justice. These young people, originally full of hopes that are generous and noble, find themselves ineffective. They will wait no more for they are already becoming fed up and disgusted, heading towards despair. They look for excitement in sex and in drugs. They see no way out for mankind. They are killing themselves.

In speaking this way of youth, I am doing so in a very general sense, for in youth can be seen all types. There are those who think only of technology, and those who enter the political parties, and those who go after money and reputation. But what is new is the vast number who burn with these new ideals, even if their motivation is sometimes a bit confused. It is they who will decide our future, and who can give, if they find a source of hope, a new breath of life to humanity.

2. THE INCREASE OF VIOLENCE AND DIVISION IN THE WORLD

Let's turn now from youth with its ideals and disillusion, towards the world as it is today with its divisions and outbreaks of violence. The world is in search of unity, it hopes for unity, but it has never seemed so divided. Let us look at some of these divisions which are the sore spots of humanity.

There are the divisions on the international plane, between the American camp, the Russian camp, and the Chinese camp. Contests of influence, armed interventions, sales of arms, whole peoples are being bought for military bases. And we are all living in constant fear of the terrible weapons owned by the big powers which are capable of annihilating the human race, not to speak of the new types of biochemical weapons shortly to become operational. The race for arms makes necessary the allotment of a huge percentage of national budgets for military purposes. The small countries, much as they claim independence, are more or less forced to join one or the other of the major camps who sell them arms, in order to defend themselves against other small countries which are given arms by someone else. The war in Vietnam, in the Middle East, sales of arms in Africa, are signs of the serious divisions which can any day erupt and explode.

National divisions, whether they be between management and labour, or between language or cultural groups, seem to grow wider. The violence in Québec, the dissatisfaction of the Flemish in Belgium, the French crisis of May, 1968, and strikes of all sorts are some of the signs of these divisions.

76

Colour barriers in the United States threaten to cause an explosion of terrible violence, a violence that will be the worse for the war experiences of young American soldiers in Vietnam. The centuries of slavery, the subordination of the blacks in a white society, cannot be regulated in a couple of years. It is not simply a question of giving a few rights, but something much more fundamental, a concept to be changed, prejudices to be eradicated. And it does not seem as if the majority in America is ready to make these changes.

Division between the rich and the poor is widening, for the rich people and countries are able to acquire more wealth more quickly than the poor countries and people. Some social groups and people are in want while others waste and amass superfluous and valuable goods. This is where hatred and jealousy are born. Revolutionary movements — particularly in South America — are being organized with more or less the support of certain international powers, to drive out the rich and powerful minority. And, greater the fear of revolution or anarchy, more the tyranny and repression.

These more visible divisions are only the signs of many other divisions that exist: between generations, between man and woman in the war of the sexes, the divisions in the very heart of man, torn between hope and despair, between life and death, faith and doubt, between love and hate, between fidelity to the spirit of God and egoism or selfishness, between good and evil, between truth and untruth, between war and peace. Man longs for the infinite and he is bogged down in the limitations of matter. He seeks the eternal, but he is chained to time. Man is a creature of extraordinary nobility made for love and sanctity, but at the same time, he is capable of decadence, hate and violence. This is the anguish of the human condition. This anguish of man faced with his own destiny is increased by the fact that he has cut himself off from the certainty of faith in revelation. It is this anguish which is one of the causes of violence in our time. This violence, without any doubt, will go on increasing in the years to come, showing itself on personal, national and international levels through delinquency, crime, revolution and war.

3. SIGNS OF HOPE

Yet there are signs of hope; one can feel an awakening. There is a search for peace and unity among churches and religions; there is co-operation between countries; there is greater understanding, it seems, of the needs of the weak and the handicapped; there is a desire to come to the aid of countries in economic difficulty; there

77

is a new ideal within certain people and especially amongst the young. But I fear that the scale is tipped heavily in favour of an increase of division, of violence, hate, fear, and despair.

The question of peace is therefore vitally important. We must rapidly lay stress on the sources of hope and we must also rally the forces of peace to help the young to commit themselves even more to dynamic action in the cause of universal brotherhood.

Perhaps one of the most disturbing signs of our times is the confusion inside the Christian churches which are supposed to give hope on both the spiritual and the human level. Are we aware of the gravity of the situation signified by the number of priests, ministers and religious leaving their ministry and calling? The young reject the churches, their structures, their ministry, their actions, as a result of this confusion.

For all the problems of our world today and for the desires of the young, the Gospel of Jesus Christ gives an answer. More than the young, Jesus fought against hypocrisy and pharisaical attitudes; more than the young, Jesus condemned the rich; more than the young, Jesus preached an ideal of brotherhood and universal peace. But Jesus was put to death by those who did not want to be brought out of their prejudices and customs by His message of universal love, and who did not want to respond to the demands of poverty necessary to follow Him and to receive His Holy Spirit.

Jesus brings the answer to the demands of our times for truth, fraternity and mystical experience. He shows that an experience of God, his Father, is possible as long as we are willing to become humble and poor and open our hearts through compassion to those in need. Jesus is the supremely authentic one who followed to the very end the logic of His message of love, accepting death, sealing by His blood, the veracity of His message.

But the tragic thing about our age is that his message has been clouded over by his so-called disciples, by their buildings and riches, and often by their "worldly wisdom"; it is clouded by the divisions between Christians, by their mediocrity and their materialism. The saints are the true disciples of Jesus; they knew, throughout the ages and in different parts of the world, how to revive faith and give hope to others. But where are the saints in our time? Why does God hide Himself from his people? Perhaps God is waiting for a gesture of poverty, love and trust from His people. Perhaps He is wating for a gesture which is a witness of their faith — not in human science and psychology, but in Him and in the gift of the Holy Spirit which alone can guide us, inspire us, strengthen us and give us His presence.

Can God answer this call as long as Christians stay attached to their national and cultural heritage, and to a life of wealth and possessions, as long as they do not turn in a radical way towards the poor and the afflicted of the world, as long as they do not seek to integrate in their lives the Gospel of Jesus and become men and women of God?

If the world is as divided and violent as it is, if the young are disillusioned, is it not because we Christians have not dared bring them the living person of Jesus humble and poor: Jesus driven by love to save all men, to the point of giving His life? The Church, unfortunately, has too often identified itself with the wealthy and not with the poor and the most rejected. Christians frequently fear the demands of their master, and have not followed Him in His poverty, necessary condition for receiving the Holy Spirit.

Without any doubt, hope lies in lives motivated by the Holy Spirit, lives that are poor and genuine, in which we renounce the values and the wisdom of the world so as to adopt the values and wisdom of God, of compassion and the Gospels. If we Christians do not follow the message of our beloved master, if we do not let ourselves be reborn and become prophets of peace, we can expect the accomplishment of the prophecies of woe of Jesus, the prophecy of those invited to the wedding feast who were too busy to come, the prophecies concerning the rich and the pharisees . . .

4. THE GRAVITY OF THE SITUATION DEMANDS
A REVOLUTION OF LOVE

The situation is serious. Violence is spreading everywhere; war is breaking out; men are manufacturing more and more arms; the prophets of peace are all too often silent. And everywhere the poor and the hungry are in misery, and the rich hide behind the walls of their possessions. Young people are lost.

It is no longer the time for reforms. It is not a question of sending a little money to developing countries or patting the head of a little black child, or making a few reforms in social legislation. Injustice has lasted too long; too many people are living under the yoke of tyranny, hunger and forced labour. They themselves are losing hope. A bloody and violent revolution is imminent unless the affluent take the initiative:

79

"The rich have a superfluous store of things", writes Gandhi, who was a prophet of peace and unity, "which they do not need, and which are therefore neglected and wasted, while millions are starved to death for want of sustenance. If each retained possession only of what he needed, no one would be in want, and all could live in contentment. As it is, the rich are discontented no less than the poor. The poor man would fain become a millionaire, and the millionaire a multi-millionaire. The rich should take the initiative in dispossession with a view to a universal diffusion of the spirit of contentment. If only they keep their own property within moderate limits, the starving will be easily fed, and will learn the lesson of contentment along with the rich."[1]

And elsewhere Gandhi writes: "A violent and bloody revolution is a certainty one day, unless there is a voluntary abdication of riches and the power that riches give, and sharing them for the common good."[2]

When will the rich, those with too much, understand? How many revolutions, and murders, will it take before they realize that they must use their wealth for the good of all? Why, O God, why are they unwilling to share in love, for universal peace, that which they will lose at their death or through revolution?

Peace . . . peace, all men aspire to peace. But peace for the man without work, who has not enough to feed his wife and children, peace for the immigrant alone without friends, peace for the people living under tyranny or in slums, is quite different from the peace sought by the affluent. For them, peace means: "Leave me in peace . . . don't touch my things." This is the peace of those satisfied with themselves and their lot, and who remain deaf to the cries of misery and of suffering humanity. This kind of peace is an undercover war which slays the afflicted by indifference. It is maybe worse than open violence, because it goes frequently under the banner of virtue. This peace is not for us. It is a crime that calls out to God for vengeance.

Neither is peace a compromise, fixing borders and external acts, a discussion that stops violence on the outside but does not stop hatred. Peace is real understanding, and more, deep respect for others. Contempt causes division and promotes jealousy, hate and violence. As long as there are men, or groups of men, or countries and races who consider themselves to be superior, and who treat

---

[1] All Men Are Brothers: Life and Thoughts of Mahatma Gandhi as told in his own words. Navajivan Publishing House, Ahmedabad, 1960 p. 168.
[2] Ibid., p. 169.

others with disdain, there will be war. Peace will not come except through a radical conversion in men, by which they will look on others without fear, as brothers to be respected. This conversion involves loving others with different qualities, different cultures, languages, habits, needs and sufferings; not wishing to impose our culture and our ideas, but allowing them to express themselves according to their own ways. Peace can come only when men and countries become humble with respect to each other, when they stop amassing armaments and drop their attitudes of superiority and aggression, in favour of an attitude of service. It is necessary to dispel rivalry so as to give birth to friendship, mutual trust, co-operation and sharing. Ghandi wrote:

"If the recognized leaders of mankind who have control over the engines of destruction were wholly to renounce their use, with full knowledge of its implications, permanent peace can be obtained. This is clearly impossible without the Great Powers of the earth renouncing their imperialistic design. This again seems impossible without great nations ceasing to believe in soul-destroying competition and to desire to multiply wants and, therefore, increase their national possessions."[3]

And what Gandhi says about nations applies to each individual person in his relation with others.

Today mankind is faced with a radical choice. Either the forces of bloody revolution are going to explode (and governments in order to prevent this violence will react by creating police states), or else the young, with hope and a certain audacity, are going to throw themselves into a revolution of love and non-violence, accepting poverty, even death for the sake of a more equal sharing of the goods of the earth, so as to show their respect for the poor and the afflicted. Their action, especially if it is followed by a vast number of people, will tip the scale decidedly to one side, avoiding revolution of blood and making this world a land of peace. The young, I am sure, are ready. It is for us to facilitate the task.

With the grace of God, and trust in the Spirit, peace is possible.

5. SOME INDICATION FOR AN EDUCATION TOWARDS PEACE

Following what has been said about the young and about the seriousness of the time, here are a few ideas which could be used to educate the young towards universal peace.

It is a must that parents, teachers and all those who hold responsibilities — themselves become men and women of peace. This

---

[3]*Ibid.,* p. 210.

means that they must be unified in themselves and that there be no contradiction between what they say and what they think and what they live. This means that they must not endeavour to safeguard their authority in an arbitrary and artficial way. They must, in their inner being, become true and genuine. Their authority must flow from this authenticity and this truth. They must radiate it through their person and not lean on their titles and functions. They must, above all, profoundly respect the young people for whom they are responsible, listening attentively to them, helping them to express themselves, admiring their ideals and their ideas, encouraging them in non-violence, standing behind them, giving them effective counsel.

They should know how to laugh with the young, be simple with them, share with them even on a personal plane, play with them; in short, they should drop the barriers of authority so as to show their real selves without fear.

If parents and teachers are unafraid, if they do not attempt to defend at any price their rank, their ideas, their mores, their ideals, their way of life, their religion, their riches, the young will feel the peace emanating from them. And they will follow them with confidence. The new form of education should be built above all on mutual trust.

To be a man of peace, the child must have lived in an atmosphere of peace and sharing. The small child is terribly sensitive. He grasps quickly the presence of division and discord. If he feels around him a climate of unity he will grow in unity and will become a unifying person. If he grows up in a climate of discord he will become an element of discord.

We radiate what we are. If the hearts of parents are at peace, they will avoid all *a priori* judgements, discriminating remarks about such and such categories of people, whether it be Africans, communists or peasants. They will resist the temptation to label, which makes classification easy but prevents the meeting of two persons in truth and liberty. Harry is not left or right, he is just Harry.

There are bits of conversations one hears in certain families which slowly but surely, almost imperceptibly — the way a sponge absorbs water — shape the child as a person. "Quick, run and get that seat before that black man gets it." "I'll be glad to help such and such a family, once they learn to say thank you." "If your friends ask you to lend them your crayons, tell them mummy doesn't want you to."

82

A child becomes peaceful himself if he hears conversations that are always warm and friendly, if those around him know how to admire, to marvel, to be grateful, if they do not criticize or make unkind judgements, if they always see the good in people, and if they can forgive others easily.

Parents and teachers should be well informed about the problems of our time, but the information must never be without hope. If educators do not have a sense of history, a sense of the unity of the world and a sense of universality, they will run the risk of not grasping the urgency of our time, and will fail to see that the answers will not come except through new, audacious and decisive action. In the field of information, governments, churches, men of letters and those in the communications media must assume fully their responsibilities. They have no right to placate public opinion by letting men continue to live in a dream world of happiness and myths when they know the truth about society. They have no right to allow men to dance at the mouth of a volcano when they know that the volcano may erupt any moment.

Information, announcing the gravity of the hour, must not be a cause of sadness and discouragement which would increase despair. Along with the information there must also be rays of hope and life and suggestions of action to be taken. While the world-wide picture of impending revolutions and violence is brought to light, the possibilities of a change towards peace must also be shown. It is essential that we show how clear-headed, generous and committed men and women are meeting the challenge, and how we can imitate them and join them in spirit.

The television screen must not show crimes, uncontrolled passions, and all that appeals to the morbid senses, nor delusions of happiness and despair, but the joyous, sometimes even heroic lives of dedicated people. We must see the marvellous generosity of those young people who have gone to work in far off countries; we must be shown the audacity of couples who give up all personal ambition in order to give themselves to others in poverty and simplicity; we must be shown the radiance of the faces of those without many material goods but who live according to other, more profound, values; we must be shown that men can be happy living in community; we must be shown that there is a possible solution for society, which is neither the tyranny of communist countries nor the materialistic liberty of capitalist countries.

The communications media, instead of being used to sell products through advertising, should be used to try to generate a new generosity and a new hope in the young, to help them to respond effectively to the violence of our time, by showing them what could be done in the way of effective non-violent action, based on sharing and brotherhood. We should even give the young the use of the airwaves, so that they themselves can announce their new and audacious message.

The young need guides and models whom they can follow. They are thirsting for that new society of brothers which alone can give real meaning to their life. They must, then, find leaders who believe in the possibility of universal peace and who, to attain this peace, will leave home, country and culture to serve the humble and the less fortunate. The new world cannot be built unless a considerable number of young people no longer barricade themselves behind the wall of materialism or even violence, and are willing to live humbly, sharing the life of the less privileged. They must have the courage to leave everything for the sake of winning the precious pearl of universal brotherhood. But to be sufficiently inspired and to persevere in following this inspiration, they must do it with some of their elders, they must find models, men and women who help them beat the path that leads to justice and peace and love of the afflicted.

And we should be able to find these guides in all walks of life. Not all can go and work in the developing countries, or leave their surroundings to live in less privileged ones; but everyone can leave their social prejudices, opening their hearts and their homes to strangers, to the handicapped and to the afflicted, unafraid of being eaten up by them. All can devote some of their vacation and leisure time to visiting the sick, or old people, or those nearby who are of another culture or who live in the slums, or those in prison. Everyone can incite and encourage the young to attempt new forms of community living, and to share in a new way with those who suffer.

Educators — if they are thus called by God — must live a spiritual life, directed to mystical experience and compassion. They must discard from religion all elements of hypocrisy. They must live the essentials of the message of Jesus: openness to the Holy Spirit, compassion for the weak and the afflicted, love of enemies, the refusal to judge or criticize others.

In this domain educators must have a deep respect for the young, whom God loves in a special way and to whom He sends His Spirit in a new way. An educator can be but a humble instrument of the Spirit, he cannot impose; his actions must resemble those of Jesus who washed His disciples' feet, and who accepted martyrdom so that others may live. He must make great demands of himself, but be full of respect and mercy, without judgement, with regards to others. And he must live fully the message of Jesus:

"Happy are you who are poor,
afflicted and persecuted!
Woe to you who are rich!
How can the love of God be in
us if our hearts are closed
to a brother in need?"

Educators must reflect with the young upon the parables of Lazarus, of the good Samaritan, of those invited to the wedding feast; they must reflect also on the identification of Jesus with the poor, on the exigency of His call, on what He says about Providence. They must ask together of Jesus that He send His Holy Spirit and His gifts, so they may receive the new force that will make them more courageous, more generous, more illuminating, more humble and more present. They must ask together audaciously and insistently for new hearts, for hearts of flesh in place of hearts of stone. Together they must, deeply united in the mystical body, joined with the pastors and the apostles, find a religion of spirit and truth, which leads them to interior liberty, the liberty of the children of God.

The child and the young person must meet the poor person and live with him.

We must bring the child, at an early age, into contact with misery, and people of different milieu, not only through books and television, but through meetings and the friendship that follows. Generally, children make no distinction of class and race; they are for the most part quite at ease amongst people of different groups; the distinctions and divisions come from their elders.

God save us from the politeness and social conventions which have for too long prevented children of different backgrounds from playing together for fear of their learning bad language, bad table manners, and of their forgetting how to behave properly. My God, when will this hypocrisy stop? When will it be understood that there is a priority of values, that it is a thousand times better to swear or to have bad table manners than to close one's heart to the poor?

Let us not be afraid that our children might play with children of poorer backgrounds. Let us not be too afraid that they might catch diseases. There is only one true disease, that of having a closed heart, a heart of stone.

If very early, a youngster is brought into contact with families of different backgrounds, or with handicapped children, a real desire to share will be born in him. One of the tragedies in our schools is that for too long the whole system has been based on the competitive spirit, and with this, a contempt for the weak. Competition is a healthy thing, but if it is not coupled with a desire for fraternity and a tolerance for the less capable, competition quickly becomes contempt, then division, then war.

If we attenuate the great importance we usually place on intelligence, and domination through intelligence, and if we try to encourage the growth of co-operation between the weak and the strong, the rich and the poor, maybe the child and the young person will discover the one true goal of wealth and intelligence: to better serve their brothers in need and thus to make a better world.

In order for the child to grow with a heart of peace and to become a maker of peace, there must be in him none of the barriers of fear which prevent men from seeing each other as brothers. He must learn to welcome others, especially those who are not like him in background, and culture and way of life. We are never afraid of those who are similar to us; it is the one who is different in wealth, or class, or rank, or political standing, or religion who seems to be a threat to our lives.

Education towards peace and openness necessitates a determined heart and solid interior convictions. It is impossible to listen to and really understand another person, especially if he is different, unless one is inhabited by a force which is at the same time strong and delicate, and which permits one to *be* without losing one's self. Without this interiority or this peace that comes from convictions, we are inconsistent, soft, and incapable of a true union of love, incapable of healing the spiritual and physical wounds of others.

This interiority is the cause and effect of the young person discovering a true personal morality, a morality of love, which surges from his inner being and flows like a source of living water. It is this morality or spirituality which gives him real interior liberty and erases all fear.

This also presupposes that the young person has a deep sense of truth, that he be educated in a love for the truth, which implies that he knows how to distinguish between the things that are absolutely essential from the things that are accessory and secondary; the certain from the probable and the possible. And above all, this implies that he is able to see in all conversations and persons, positive and true elements which allow for a working together — not value judgements, or discussions where one

86

wants to prove one is right. It is only then that he can appreciate the real value and thoughts of others.

CONCLUSION

To be a man of peace, one must know how to clothe every action and every word in the garments of peace, of non-aggressivity and of non-violence. In this domain Mahatma Gandhi is among the greatest masters. We of the West have much to learn from him. Here I will quote only a few of his reflections, but it is important that all of us read his works:

"Non-violence is 'not a resignation from all real fighting against wickedness'. On the contrary, the non-violence of my conception is a more active and real fight against wickedness than retaliation whose very nature is to increase wickedness. I contemplate a mental and therefore a moral opposition to immoralities." [4]

"Non-violence is a power which can be wielded equally by all — children, young men and women or grown up people — provided they have a living faith in the God of Love and have therefore equal love for all mankind. When non-violence is accepted as the law of life it must pervade the whole being and not be applied to isolated acts." [5]

"In my opinion non-violence is not passivity in any shape or form. Non-violence as I understand it, is the most active force in the world . . . Non-violence is the supreme law." [6]

"In its positive form, *ahimsā* means the largest love, greatest charity. If I am a follower of *ahimsā* I must love my enemy. I must apply the same rules to the wrong-doer who is my enemy, or a stranger to me, as I would to my wrong-doing father or son. This active *ahimsā* necessarily includes truth and fearlessness. As man cannot deceive the loved one, he does not fear or frighten her. Gift of life is the greatest of all gifts; a man who gives it in reality, disarms all hostility. He has paved the way for an honourable understanding. And none who is himself subject to fear can bestow that gift. He must therefore be himself fearless. A man cannot practice *ahimsā* and be a coward at the same time. The practice of *ahimsā* calls forth the greatest courage." [7]

The man of peace cannot value social ambition or wealth. The man of peace does not try to dominate, to defend his property and

[4] *Ibid.*, p. 121.
[5] *Ibid.*, p. 118.
[6] *Ibid.*, p. 126.
[7] *Ibid.*, p. 120.

to prove his superiority. The man of peace is necessarily humble; he seeks to call peace into the heart of every man. He is there to communicate that which is most precious: love and peace. Then very quickly he discovers the link between peace and poverty: material poverty as well as spiritual poverty. "If we are to be non-violent, we must then not wish for anything on this earth which the meanest or the lowest of human beings cannot have," wrote Gandhi.[8]

All this implies that the child and the young person must learn little by little to put their faith not in knowledge for the service of power or social rank, but in the supreme goods which are compassion, understanding of men, a thirst for justice, in order to become a healer of men. They must discover the immense love of God for man and put their whole confidence in Him.

> "I am in the world feeling my way to light 'amid the encircling gloom'. I often err and miscalculate . . . My trust is solely in God. And I trust men only because I trust God. If I had no God to rely upon, I should be, like Timon, a hater of my species."[9]

> "I must go . . . with God as my only guide. He is a jealous Lord. He will allow no one to share his authority. One has, therefore, to appear before Him in all one's weakness, empty-handed and in a spirit of full surrender, and then He enables you to stand before a whole world and protects you from all harm."[10]

The man of peace will certainly be a solitary man, but he will have found the one friend who will guide and help him, and give him strength when none is left him; his Father and Beloved God. It is only when the heart of man has found this eternal source of divine wealth that he will be able to perfectly renounce all possessions which divide men between themselves.

Today violence and hate abound; the young are turning to drugs and despair; mankind is at the edge of the abyss.

But there is hope. This hope is with the young who are discovering non-violence with all that it implies.

> Gandhi wrote: "In this age of wonders no one will say that a thing or idea is worthless because it is new. To say it is impossible because it is difficult, is again not in consonance with the spirit of the age. Things undreamt of are daily being seen, the impossible is ever becoming possible. We are constantly being

[8]*Ibid.*, p. 118.
[9]*Ibid.*, p. 95.
[10]*Ibid.*, p. 88.

astonished these days at the amazing discoveries in the field of violence. But I maintain that far more undreamt of and seemingly impossible discoveries will be made in the field of non-violence."[11]

When death and hate are everywhere, when violence and aggression seem to be more and more universal, when traditions, which maintained a certain order and morality, are dropped; when we see breaking loose after liberation from the shackles of tradition, instincts of destruction and the search for egotistical pleasures; it is then that the Spirit of God is nearest. The Spirit does not hover only over quiet waters, but even more over the storm. Are we ready to listen to the follies of love and of actions in favour of justice, peace and universal brotherhood that the Spirit might inspire men for the healing of the world: Jesus, Prince of Peace, came to give us His Peace, leave us His Peace, and to make us men of Peace.

In conclusion, I will quote Pope Paul VI in his encyclical, "Progressio Populorum" in which he himself quotes his humble and esteemed predecessor John XXIII.

> "The prayer of all ought to rise with fervour to the Almighty so that the human race, having become aware of such great misfortunes, will apply itself with intelligence and steadfastness to abolish them. This prayer should be matched by the resolute commitment of each individual — according to the measure of his strength and possibilities — to the struggle against underdevelopment. May individuals, social groups, and nations join hands in brotherly fashion, the strong aiding the weak to grow, exerting all their competence, enthusiasm and love to the task. For he who is animated by true charity labours skillfully to discover the cause of misery, to find the means to combat it, to overcome it resolutely. A creator of peace will 'continue in his path, lighting lamps of joy and playing their brilliance and loveliness on the hearts of men across the surface of the globe, leading them to recognize, across all frontiers, the faces of their brothers, the faces of their friends'."

---

[11]*Ibid.*, p. 144.

My Flesh For Peace

Peace
a thirst for unity
fusion
a calling forth of my being
my entrails
to be united
and unite
in the flames of the infinite . . .

surge forth in creativity
erupting in peace
living waters
that gently flow
delicately healing
the wounds of despisal
and division.

Can I take into my flesh
your sadness, despair
your violence even, which **jaggers** *forward*
from so many years of rejection.

Your crushed hands
and burnt out eyes
your empty belly
your feeling of uselessness
your solitude
your terrible feeling of aloneness
because I . . . and others like me . . .
have looked down upon you with disdain
from our man-made
stature.

I know your violence or despair
or the depths of your lethargy
your love of self-centred pleasure.
But is my thirst for peace
as forceful as your thirst for violence
jaggering *forward from anguish?*
as deep as your lethargy, love of pleasure, or despair?

Can my thirst for peace
and your violence
embrace
unite
make love
your violence awakening me
exciting me
urging me forth
to life
my thirst for peace
— yes, mingling with cowardice, fear —
(my God heal this cowardice and fear
make me an instrument of your peace)
calling your violence to a new form of action

"Just as one must learn the art of killing in the training
for violence, so must one learn the art of dying in the
training for non-violence. Violence does not mean
emancipation from fear, but discovering the means of
combatting the cause of fear. Non-violence, on the other
hand, has no cause for fear. The votary of non-violence
has to cultivate the capacity for sacrifice of the highest
type in order to be free from fear. He recks not if he
should lose his land, his wealth, his life. He who has
not overcome all fear cannot practise *ahimsā* to per-
fection. The votary of *ahimsā* has only one fear, that is
of God. He who seeks refuge in God ought to have a
glimpse of the *atma* that transcends the body; and the
moment one has a glimpse of the imperishable *atma*
one sheds the love of the perishable body."[12]

I love you and your violence
for you have courage
not fearing death
you reject all that I reject
hypocrisy
static security in possessions
complacency
indifference in face of so many afflicted.

---

[12]*Ibid.*, p .110.

If I could have but some of your courage.
  I thirst for unity
    and need some of your audacity
      which so often I lack:
        no compromise,
        my God, help me never to make alliances
        with forces of possession and human securities
        but go forth with you
        in love
        to give my flesh with you, Jesus.
        in the struggle against hate, evil, egoism,
            for **peace:**
            complacency, injustice

And I believe in you: that you will give me
  this force
  and humility to be your instrument
    the world is crying out in thirst.

Who will give it water?
I hear the cries of anger from so many in affliction
  the groans of despair from so many

    Who is listening?
    Who will answer?

      Will you give your flesh?

Do you know that that is why you have flesh?

    not for miserable
    nights
    of man-made excited pleasure
    the curse of sexual comings and goings
    vomiting taboos
      in despairing nakedness
    drunken love which soils the name
    orgies of kisses
      reeking of death
      smell of urine
      sweat

93

But a flower
    opening slowly
        gracefully
            answering your silent call
            giving delicate petals
            and seeds for life
        a scent that embalms
            an incense
                calling me forth
                to a new form of violence
                the violence of silence
                giving my flesh
                to heal rejections
                    urging men to live
                    as brothers
                    taking them into my flesh.

Will they find in my flesh,
    your Spirit, Jesus
or do they find my pride
    which is death?

Your Spirit,
Your Spirit, Jesus.

Did you know that you have life
        . . . to give it?

> "Non-violence is the greatest force at the disposal of mankind. It is mightier than the mightiest weapon of destruction devised by the ingenuity of man. Destruction is not the law of the humans. Man lives freely by his readiness to die, if need be, at the hands of his brother, never by killing him. Every murder or other injury, no matter for what cause, committed or inflicted on another is a crime against all humanity."[13]

---

[13]*Ibid.*, p. 110.

Community of Men and Women of Peace

who will promise:

— to live according to Gandhiji's[1] principle of *ahimsā,* that is to say, non-violence, humility of heart and a desire to bring justice and peace to this world, not by violent means and bloody revolution, but by a strong and effective love by which they work constantly and even offer themselves in sacrifice to conquer injustice, hate, and evil, seeking always to unify men, calling them forth to gift of self and to be brothers.

— to live this principle of *ahimsā* by refusing to judge, criticize, or condemn another; by refusing all divisions and barriers based on or provoking fear, spite, disdain, or feelings of superiority or inequalities of wealth and opportunity; by trying always to see and respect all that is positive in their brother and in the differences which exist, in order to build wth all men a better world, trying always to unite all men, groups and nations in truth, and justice, and love.

— to live poorly, simply, and without affectation, giving away at least their superfluous goods to the needy of the world, in order to spread a spirit of contentment and peace amongst all; and where it is possible, seeking to live together as brothers with the afflicted and impoverished in communities of peace and hope.

— to trust in God, Father of all men, source of all love and of all peace; seeking constantly to live in His Presence, in a spirit of prayer, breathing His Beloved Name; accepting and seeking poverty in spirit; appearing helpless and weak before Him in order to be inhabited by His divine strength and to be available to act at all times as His instrument of creative love and unifying peace; each

« Maison d'Emmanuel »   « La Merçi »   « L'Hermitage »
60 - TROSLEY-BREUIL   16 - COURBILLAC   60 - AUTRECHES
        France   France   France
[1]Gandhi.

95

seeking to live according to that belief through which God seems to call him, with all its exigencies of mystical union, liberty in the Spirit and compassion for the impoverished and for one's enemies, worshipping according to the liturgy and rites of his religion, in a spirit of openness, wonderment and love for one another.

— to seek to live in truth in all their thoughts, acts and relationships to others, not pretending to be other than they are by hiding their faults, weaknesses and deficiencies, but desiring to be really themselves, confident, nevertheless, that they are capable of living in ever greater truth because God, who is Truth, in His fantastic love, dwells within them.

— to work consciously and effectively in this spirit of *ahimsā* as the instrument of the God of Truth and Love, as peacemakers who seek to destroy, if necessary in their own flesh, the barriers that separate men and prevent them from loving in freedom and without fear; thus they can help to create a world of joy, unity and wonderment where all men can celebrate the marvels of life which spring from the very heart of God, their Beloved Father.

The World In Violence: Eruption To Hope?

It is now over twenty years since I left the Armed Forces —
where I had been trained in gunnery, letting off torpedos and
dropping depth charges. From this world of parade and what I
would call "controlled" violence for the maintenance of order, I
have been called little by little into another world. I was trained
in a traditional school of thought where position, honesty and
order went hand in hand. As the years have gone by, certain
barriers which were created by these seemingly human values have
dropped. And I find myself, day by day, more and more closely
linked to Raphael at l'Arche, or Gurunathan who is in Asha
Niketan, our home in India, and to all their brothers, be they at
l'Arche, or Daybreak, or la Merci, or Asha Niketan, or the world
over. They are in a very different world to that which seems to be
evolving through the economies and industries of the world,
through publicity and the mass media. When people ask me, as
they do quite frequently, "Is it not depressing to live with mentally
deficient people?", I realize that I am becoming more closely
linked every day to the so-called abnormal rather than to the
so-called normal, who are the masters of this world, of its economy,
and of the decisions that affect populations.

Recently, I was in India, and was able to visit the slums of
Bombay and of Madras. With a few friends, we started a little
home in Bangalore in order to bring some peace and hope and
work to a few men wounded in their minds and nervous systems.
I was able to appreciate the style of life, the spirituality and the
culture of India. From the eyes of young Indian children, with
radiant skin, bare feet and no toys, I returned to Paris and the
overlit shops of Christmas-tide: a world of luxury that had forgotten the unfortunate ones of the world, forgotten the meaning of
Christmas.

---

1 Talk given to the Empire Club of Canada, February 11, 1971.

97

The other day at Trosly, a boy of twenty-six arrived, sent to us from Belgium. I will call him Peter but that isn't his real name. He came from a broken family. He had not worked much in his life and there were certainly some personality disorders coming from a deep frustration of love. He wore all his worldly possessions — a suit of clothes, a shirt: no money, no suitacse. I asked him if he had any friends. He said, "No." He had gone from institution to institution. He had been in psychiatric hospitals, in prison for vagrancy. Alone — terribly alone. He had no place to go. He had not asked to live, he had not chosen his misfortune, and in talking with me, he seemed to want to call down death. Yet he had a deeply calling smile, an innocent look, a childlike need of affection and tenderness, but he is from a poor, divided and violent world. He went to the South of France, returned, committed some strange acts, shouted a bit, was shoved into a psychiatric hospital where he was shut up in a cell and pumped with drugs. A lonely boy facing a frightened society. Peter was crippled and wounded. And society with its clean conscience continues. While we eat today, I think of Peter, I think of the wounded and the despised the world over, and of the children of India. Because of them, I am beginning to sense the vast division of our world.

On one side, men hiding themselves in comfort and in security, the securities of wealth, of possessions, of clubs and of drink. Here we have in many ways the makers of this world: those who have made good and are sitting on the crest of success. Their eyes are glued to wealth and domination and social esteem. They may be men of morality or immorality; they may have had their way blessed, journeying more or less in harmony with religious groups. Their conscience may be clear because they have put a few bills in the beggar's hat that is offered to them from the poor quarters of their own city, or even from far-off countries. They live in a world of luxury, of superfluous goods, of snobbishness, of expensive houses and motor cars, of well-fed children with beautiful well-brushed hair and well-cleaned finger nails, who are going to good schools and are heading, maybe, towards the same crest of success where they, too, will be able to open bank accounts.

On the other side, another world, a world of the handicapped and of the broken, those who are on welfare, who slug down the streets or are shut up in prisons or psychiatric hospitals, who may have taken to drugs and drink and prostitution. Go to the big homes for the mentally and physically handicapped, the psychiatric hospitals and the prisons, and find out where you might be if you had had that sickness or virus at the age of four, if you had been hit by a cyclist when very young, or if you had been born in a world of squalor and violence. You will see then what I mean by the sadness of loneliness.

We are entering into a new stage in the history of humanity: the age of moon exploration, supersonic aircraft, nuclear energy, electronics, computers and television. Man, though he is still enclosed in time, is no longer shut in by space. The world which, until a few years ago, was like a well-ordered piece of furniture in which there was a multiplicity of self-contained drawers, has now become like a vast interacting machine, where people and cultures and ideas are being mingled. Technically, man has grown within a few years from a tiny child to an adult. We have at our fingertips terrific powers and yet we are just at the beginning of discovery. The unimagined of a few years is becoming reality. There has been an amazing evolution in the discoveries of artificial power and energy, but in our style of living and in our hearts, we do not seem to progress — perhaps we are even regressing.

One of the consequences of the advances in communications is precisely the unification of the despised and of the impoverished. That is why we will be seeing more and more violence amongst those who for too long have been looked down upon in the ghettos of Harlem or the tragic slums of South America, and elsewhere. It is not possible for the proud and the wealthy to remain any longer despising and indifferent, alongside empty stomachs, the oppressed, the handicapped and the lonely. Today, through mass media, radio and television, the empty stomachs of the world are gathering together in face of the luxury and wastage of others. In the knowledge of inequalities of wealth and opportunity, in front of so many injustices and tyranny, it will not take too long for the empty stomachs and the oppressed to spring into action.

The refusal to understand the sufferings of others flows quickly into contempt and tyranny. And these are at the source of all divisions, violence and hatred. Why have some men power and domination, frequently springing only from the good fortune of birth, whilst others are in misery, powerless, unhappy? Why do those in power despise the powerless? When will they understand that, if they have wealth and power, it is to share with those who have nothing?

These two worlds of opulence and misery divide not only the globe, but also every one of our cities and our countries. The arrogant and the opulent, sometimes paternalistically benevolent, accuse the others of laziness and stupidity. But it is their arrogance and egoism which stimulate a desire for revenge or else incite to despair and death. Also the handicapped are unable to manifest

99

their discontent; they have no voice and cannot express themselves; they have no power. But this duality must not, and cannot, continue.

The world is in many ways becoming unified. And religious
tradition and morality are not just waning, they are near death.
An alliance between the opulent and the so-called religious world
was formed early in history. But prophets and saints were cruci-
fied, or lived on the margin of society. They were laughed at and
mocked; their teachings or way of life were considered imprudent
and impossible. Men have too long refused the Beatitudes and the
Sermon on the Mount. Reason seems to most men to be greater
and more productive than the foolishness of the Spirit.

The regional and national traditions of religion, of morality and
of styles of life, which gave a certain cohesion to national groups
are collapsing through the influences of mingling cultures. In face
of this breakdown of mores, some cry out victory: man is liberated
from the taboos of religion! Others, seeing the developing movement of anarchy and of free sexuality, weep for man's decadence.
With the disappearance of tradition, with all forms of authority
being questioned, man finds himself tragically alone. There is no
certitude concerning ultimate questions of life and death, of love
and hate, of hope and despair, of good and evil. In his unquench-
able thirst for a universal truth and beauty, for a meaning for
existence, man discovers he is lost and in anguish. This very
anguish makes him jagger forth in unlimited quests for wealth and
ambition. Having lost inner security and peace, he looks desperately for other compensations: the compensation of exterior wealth.
Or else, this anguish, faced with the meaningless values and injustices of our society of consumption, incites him to other experiences which help him to escape from drudgery into a world of
drugs and sexuality or into a world of excitement and violence
and delinquency. Against rebellious youth, men of order and of
wealth, reclining in private property, cry out in horror, just as
white people condemn the outbreaks of violence in Harlem. They
have not realized the violence of their attitudes and of their proud
selfishness.

We must not give birth to children (we cannot be just like
rabbits procreating little rabbits), unless we take the pulse of this
world, diagnose its sickness and try to make for our children a
better world. It is tragic to beget children and unleash them into
a world of violence and despair which has lost all meaning. We
must try to make for them a better world. We cannot close our
eyes to the most serious of all problems, these divisions between
the smug and the despised, the divisions between continents. If

we do, we will be overwhelmed by the anger of rising countries or of the oppressed who will face our flagging motivation with dynamism. We will be submerged by a youthful army wandering aimlessly and without guidance around our countries.

We are confronted by the problems of hunger and over-production, by world tensions and possibilities of conflagration, by unhappy young people in search of meaning and rejecting hypocrisy and false values. If we, who are men of power and wealth, who command the mass media and the economy of our country, if we do not act rapidly and decisively, we can be sure that we will be drowned in the tidal waves of violence or despair. It is too late just to give out paternalistic gifts, to pat the heads of children in the slums of India. Something more real and profound must be done. We need men of courage who will follow the logic of their inner beliefs, who give up a style of life which separates them from their fellow men and who adopt a life of real compassion and of sharing.

Gandhi said the world has made fantastic strides in the discovery and usages of violence and he was certain that we are on the brink of fantastic discoveries in the domain of love and of non-violence.

To bring peace to this divided world, we must find new means which can match the new discoveries of science and of violence. We must break through our old styles and ways of life to create communities of friends where hierarchy is based not on birth, heritage, wealth and frequently unmerited position, but upon personal values of inner depth, life of the spirit and love and compassion. It is no longer the time to give away some superfluous wealth; we must give much more, and we must even change our lives in order to create communities of friends where friendship and compassion are treasured over individual power, wealth and ambition. The day must come — if it doesn't, we will all be smothered by an overwhelming movement of violence and despair — when men of business must share with their workers as brothers and not just as paternalistic benefactors, when lawyers and doctors and many other professional men must live amongst the poorer members of their community creating friendly and mutually confident relationships. The day must come when many families will leave their present way of life to break down the barriers of contempt and ignorance and open their hearts to the suffering ones of their city and through them, to the suffering ones of the world. The day must come when instead of creating large walls around our houses, we open large doors to welcome at our table the lonely, the old and the handicapped. The young are impatient, and rightly so. They have had enough of those who have given lip service to a God who was obviously not the Living God of love. They have had enough of those who for too long have prayed in their fashionable hats, in front of the most despised of men, crowned with thorns and covered with spittle — the irony of Christianity which kneels on velvet cushions in front of a Jesus condemned for blasphemy, rejected by the people. The young have had enough of those who value only social esteem and money. They are desperately impatient for a new experience which places an absolute in sincerity and rejects all hypocrisy. If we believe in God, we must follow this inner belief and meet this God of love and of mercy and of tenderness and of justice. It is He who calls forth in us a dynamism of the Spirit and who breaks down the barriers which have been built up on our land of fear.

Out of an erupting world, a world that is being unified technically but which remains so drastically divided, a new force will be born which will match the violence and give life to growing despair.

Our hope is in the young, in their quest for authenticity, in their openness and tolerance. But, if they do not find men and women, their elders, who are ready to seek love and compassion above individual wealth and possessions, then these young people will fall into despair or non-productive, suicidal activities. In face of a rising revolution of violence or the tidal wave of despair and escapism, we must inspire a revolution of love and compassion where our energies and intelligence, capacities and technical resources are put to the service of bringing peace and justice to our fellow men and especially to those in misery and sadness.

But where are we to find the energy and strength to turn our hearts of stone into hearts of flesh, to break down the barriers of fear which we build around ourselves? How can we destroy prejudices and attitudes of contempt which prevent us from communicating with those who are suffering and who are our brothers — be they in China, India, Africa or Harlem, in the luxurious apartments of Toronto or in the Northwest Territories.

Only the Spirit of God can give us the strength to pass from the world of egoism and of acquisition to the world of understanding, of sharing and of sacrifice: only the Spirit of Love can transform our hearts of stone to hearts of flesh and tender compassion.

My message is a call, a call which finds its source in the eyes of those children I saw in India, in the eyes of the handicapped of the world, and of all those who are suffering and whose voices are not heard. May the Spirit of God who loves each one of us, use my poor words to delve into your hearts so that you may discover the riches of a life given to the service of our fellow men, so that our world may become a haven of peace — a garden and not a jungle. May the Spirit of God teach each one of us that the greatness of life comes not in acquiring, but in dispossessing, and in sharing: not in stifling life, but in giving life.

May God change my heart and yours, giving to each one of us the courage to become men of Peace, prophets of Peace. I mean a peace which is not slumber in satisfaction and wealth, fearful of wars and revolution, but a sharing in dynamic unity like a vast and marvellous symphony. In this peace, all men, rich or poor, black or white, handicapped or not, participate in the same universal and fraternal love which is but the sign of that great wedding feast of eternal love and joy to which we are all convened when our days are finished and when time dies in the birth of eternity.

As My Heart Opens Up

As my heart opens up

  under your touch

    I hear your call to death Jesus

      faint,

        whispering in peace

          offering my flesh in sacrifice

           waiting,

            waiting tenderly for my hour

          knowing that I am

        hidden

      in the hand

     the heart

    the womb

   of your father

  I await in silence

the wedding.